**APPLYING
BUDDHA'S
TEACHINGS
IN MODERN SOCIETY**

APPLYING BUDDHA'S TEACHINGS IN MODERN SOCIETY

by THICH NU TINH QUANG

Thich Nu Tinh Quang

Applying

BUDDHA'S TEACHINGS

IN MODERN SOCIETY

A Thesis Presented For the Degree of Ph. D
in Religious Studies

UNITED BUDDHIST PUBLISHER (UBP)

CONTENTS

1. INTRODUCTION

"Ethics is the immune system of a humane society."

- Frederic Reamer

Today society is facing with its ethical problems. Religious function of Religion play more have more roles than at any time for contributing to build a society of order, stability and peace on the earth. This time, the actually Buddha's teachings are not the application of the Buddhist community only, but to existence of human kind in general. Those are ecological risks, such as pollution, finiteness of natural resources, progressing diseases, risk of the mass murder using nuclear weapon, all kinds of dependencies, from drugs to Internet, consumerism, terrorism, the problem of the Third World, and so on. Due to the acceleration of the technological progress, the risk is growing every year in a geometrical progression, and because of that, now it is extremely important to look for solutions in the ancient wisdom that proved to be immortal and true. The Buddha's teaching is one of those heritages of humankind that can serve as a cure of a new society.

In Buddhist worldview, human beings live in the illusion of separateness while their true nature is single with the whole universe. We are all a single living organism with interrelated and integrated physically, spiritually and locally. But majority of mankind is still ignorant of that fact, and acts egoistically so as we all were separated. Most people act egoistically, following their delusional vain passions from suffering, in which they live, and deepening their suffering even more in their fussy races for the desires. The problem is their actions (along with our words and thoughts) not only do harm to themselves but to every part of the being at the same time. For that reason, many people in the world are suffering, animals and plants are suffering, and the planet Earth itself is suffering.

The Buddha was the one who intended to stop all that suffering and suggested a teaching where he instructed how to do it. In this research, I will examine the Buddha's teaching and teachings of his followers concerning in which way those teachings can be a cure for a new world's society, and how could it solve our global problems and ease the suffering of people who live in the digital world of the twenty-first century.

The topics I will consider in this paper are following. I will briefly consider the major problems of nowadays society and the basic principles of Buddhist philosophy concerning the existence of human beings. Then we will research the Buddhist perspective on the problem of violence and the methods of preventing it suggested by the Buddha himself and his followers. After that, I will discuss the five moral precepts of the Buddha and the Buddhist moral principles in general. The next stage of the research will be the analysis of the Eightfold Path suggested by Buddhists and how this path may lead to a salvation of every living being. The final part of the paper will be dedicated to the application of Buddhist philosophy and ethics to the global world issues specifically for every sphere of life. In the end, I will sum up gathered information and make a conclusion on my topic.

The methodology I will use is analyzing the original texts, academic critique, and the words of Buddhist key figures on the topics that I included in my research. After that on every stage of the working process I will apply the information I gathered to the problems of modern society and define the ways in which this application is possible and useful. For that part, I will use both our critical thinking and external literature.

2. TODAY SOCIETY AND ITS PROBLEMS

Today the vast majority of options which speak of this of another freedom, and freedom is being understood in some kind of defective way. It is assumed, for example, that you are free if you are able to make business, and your state does not interfere with your work, or another example: you are free when there are no proprietors standing above you. All these notions of freedom suggest the presence of some criterion, the feasibility of which one determines the difference between freedom and unfreedom, assumed human desire to have a certain ability or right or advance his well-known and supposedly coveted, and after founding this opportunity, he becomes completely free. In fact, the concept of freedom is formulated by analogy with a completely different concept, and having nothing similar to freedom; however, the concept underlying the system of values of modern civilization - term needs. There is a certain need, as long as you deny it, you are not free, but if you will satisfy it - you are free! In modern civilization there is no notion of freedom as a universal concept, as a concept; the meaning of which is determined by the human inner being and state of freedom is fixed not by external criteria, but by the personality itself.

Human is a dualistic creation; materialism and spirituality coexist inside of every person. Fighting between two sides of human nature is fully reflected in the teachings of all the great spiritual leaders, not only the Buddha's, but also in other ones. In particular, Buddhists, Christians and Judaism, etc., have developed rules governing the economic activities in such a way that each sought to satisfy not only personal own needs, but also the needs of the community.

These are the idea of the 'compassion' in Buddhism, the idea of the love of neighbor in Christianity and in Judaism Mitzvah. All the mankind history can be considered as the struggle between the forces of selfish materialism and the voice of justice and compassion.

2.1 CONSUMERISM

One of the facts, which characterize current stage of humanity development, is the creation of different new devices and progressive technologies aimed to improve the comfort of human existence. But while for some people new social benefits are becoming more and more widely available, for the other part of human race the inability to take all of the advantages of new goods has already became a sign of their social backwardness. Thus, inequality in consumption standards has already become one of the most important criteria of social differentiation nowadays.

Poor people are trying to reach the consumption level of the rich ones, for whom such aspiration is obviously; that is why they became rich. In such way, achieving unlimited consumption is the one thing everybody wants and tries to reach this goal, and using his own capabilities. High consumption standards like this are strongly propagated by media, as the desired pattern of ordinary lifestyle. This universal desire nourishes and supports some kind of pyramid that forming a vicious circle of desire to increase consumption all over the world. Following this path humankind has been splatted into several billions of individuals, and each of whom is fighting only for their own 'well-being' often forgetting that it may not coincide with general interests. All of us are used to criticize divided into classes' society of the feudal system; however, if we will try to analyze these disturbing trends of social stratification and group isolation, which are growing in today's society, we will surely come to conclusion that in fact, not much has changed, just several things has been renamed and served to us in slightly modified form. On this basis, the whole attitude to the sphere of things was completely changed. In the condition of mass production, constant pressure, and the absence of the interest in realities of a higher order, things that seemed to be under our control, broke in foreground, invisibly starting to control us, and cluttering the path of imagination of the modern humanity. There have always been greedy people but materialism, consumerism, and fetishization of wealth and comfort which associated with them is undoubtedly a feature of our time. Even modern art with its various directions is not interested in human and his nature anymore, admiring only things - they are old and new, broken and intact, and posed in the usual way or pilled on each other. First of all, modern individual wants to consume a lot and well, even such futile aspiration could have been nice if it would not became an end in itself; the only inexhaustible and constantly growing desire of a modern human. The one who fixated on consumption, he (she) eventually become unable to share with environment either external or internal domains. Rabid consumers only know how to 'consume' other people's abilities, their support, their services, but the one thing, from which humanity is moving away, is ability to love and mercy to each other.

Apparently, we are not only striving to satisfy our selfish desires, but also hardly trying to create more and more new objects to desire. John Kenneth Galbraith, famous American economist, in his work "The Affluent Society" (1958) points out that this strange aspect of our new economic structure is one of the main factors that distinguish it from all other economic systems, known in history. "So it is that if production creates the wants it seeks to satisfy, or if the wants emerge pari passu (concurrent) with the production, then the urgency of the wants can no longer be used to defend the urgency of the production. Production only fills a void that it has itself created," (Galbraith) claims Galbraith. After this, John says that economists (but I would say, whole humanity in general) have failed to pay due attention to the fact how important in our time the process of creating requirements and especially creating them in such excessively and thoughtlessly way we used to. It still believed that all needs arise by themselves, and people are still doing not experiencing any doubt to seeking the means of satisfying those needs.

The more we are trying to satisfy our desires - the stronger they get. This idea, at first glance, seems to contradict common sense in today's society. On the other hand, does anybody can argue that disappointment of unmet acute desire to go on a vacation to a ski resort would be less than hunger pangs, for example? As soon as person met the main necessities of life, it immediately meets the other ones. Creating new needs, we are creating new inner conflicts. Demons live inside of us; they embody lust, uncontrollable thirst to meet the needs, and to satisfy them immediately, in turn, gives a rise to a new thirst.

2.2 SLAVES ON THE MONEY

Another one important problem of the human being, which is chasing it for years, is a human's desire for money and some kind of power they could give. To buy all this things we offer in return everything we have our bodies, our time, our peace of mind, our love, and anything it requires. But sometimes we forget that all those things are totally artificial needs and what is representing an irresistible desire to meet us is money. We cannot say, that nowadays this problem became more tangible than it was earlier, but it makes the problem even more serious; since it has been entrenched in our minds for such a long time, and thus to get rid of it would be even harder. At all of the times, this one defect has been a hallmark of many people suffered from, pushing them to the terrible things, not just about themselves, but often about their surroundings.

In the past of western traditional worldview, the relationships between our spiritual obligations and material desire were regulated by regulate organized religion. As soon as spirituality ceased to be an important element of ourselves, our sense of self has increasingly become defined by the material lust, greed and addiction. Equilibrium has been violated and nowadays materialistic motives are out of control. Today the money is the main reflection of the material world, the 'profane' world, whose roots are situated deeply inside of our physical needs of the body, and inside our lusts and fears. It is starting to become totally opportune to the spirituality - reflection of our best properties, our ability to feel sorry for the other, our ability of searching for meaning of life, and the desire for unity and communion.

2.3 DRUG ADDICTION

Among all the typical addictions for the human kind which are another great problem of our day society; one of its most expressive representations is drug addiction. Vast majority are very much aware that medication habit is an interminable malady brought on by the utilization of synthetic substances that change human awareness. To a great degree quick creates reliance on infusing drug use, and this reliance is extremely troublesome treatable. Amid every medication someone who is addicted includes a dozen of individuals in the utilization procedure. Addiction because of the utilization of opiate medications is totally corrupted. Normally starts with frivolous robbery at home and after that go to asking, prostitution, and criminal strategies for cash looks. They did not stop before any strategy for extraction of cash required for the purchase of the following measurements.

Drug compulsion - an infection of the spirit, brain and body, also, if the physical reliance can at present be anything but difficult to win and to conquer the mental reliance is practically unimaginable. Be that as it may, it is conceivable to suspend and therefore effectively battle with him (her) for this illness. So in today's current restoration focuses rather effectively battle such sicknesses; despite the fact that the rate of recuperations is not high. In such organizations building up an extraordinary individual treatment approaches, which are basically coordinated not to battle the utilization, and the way that individuals could deal with their dependence and figure out how to live with it without coming back to medication use. All the time after treatment at recovery focuses the individual comes back to an ordinary life and turns into a full individual from society. As indicated by UN specialists, the aggregate turnover of the worldwide medication industry is assessed at around four hundred billion dollars. US every year, which by large, is around eight per cent of the turnover of all universal exchange. Furthermore, if a comparative example will happen and its advancement, the compulsion will keep on growing. A consequence of its movement is social and physical debasement of the dynamic populace. There is probably habit is principally a social issue. Persons taking opiate drugs, devastating themselves as people, and while likewise created unsalvageable mischief to society. The principal individuals feel the impacts of the conduct of someone who is addicted in his family and nearest company. The life of friends and family turns into a horrendous experience. They attempt futile to battle against fixation of medication, attempting to cure them, are compelled to pay obligations to contain them. In all cases, the utilization of medications prompts criminal wrongdoings such as burglaries, debauches, and even murders.

2.4 VIOLENCE AND MEDIA

In today's world, the concept of violence could not surprise anyone. It seems that due to the constant progress; violence has had to remain in the annals of history long time ago, yet every year (or even every day) we hear about more and more atrocities committed by various organizations or individuals. So the next question sounds like "Is the violence really necessary in our time?" Perhaps in the early stages of human development, violence had a certain sense; however, this no way should become a tradition.

News related to violence are one among most popular on TV. Thereby, every day we receive a lot of information about those or other acts of violence from all around the world. As strange as it may sound, but in practice, the rejection of violence does not seems so necessary to many representatives of humankind. From time to time people have resorted to this method for a variety reasons: the desire for power or the desire of money, the discrimination of other people for whatever principles, and religious-based violence which are the list going on for a long time. In the long run, a lot of people made a great profit on it. Is the whole meaning of what is happening composed in questions related to money?

Famous Slovenian psychoanalytic philosopher Slavoj

Žižek, in his book "Violence: Six Sideways Reflections", divides violence into two types: they are the objective and the subjective violence. By his definition, subjective violence is just the "tip of the iceberg"; however, exactly this is the violence we used to see we see it every day on TV: various armed conflicts, murders, terrorist attacks, rapes, and so on. Generally accepted preventive measures for such things is an immediate response in the same or even more cruel form, which is approved, and moreover, encouraged by society (for example, various anti-terroristic operations). Žižek claims that the definition of violence is impossible without the concept of zero-strap, which takes account, on the background of which the manifestation of violence would be clearly visible. The objective violence is that zero-strap - systematic violence, which is a 'normal' result of the work of our political, economic, and so on system. This bar is constantly rising under the able leadership of the global control, so many things are perceived quite as they should not be. Using the regular reports of those or another atrocities in various parts of the world, the media are pushing us to immediate response, and leaving us no time to reflect and take a critical look at the situation, so we could determine the true cause and effect. If before the media appeared, people were forced to react on violence only within their own environment; now we have to react on events all around the world. In addition, those events which lightened in the news, initially subject to censorship, and imposing us by their vision of the situation. Thus, in today's world, a person is a hostage of information prison.

Žižek shows us how skillfully media who are drawing our attention to some things and says nothing about the other ones that have cheated us. The reason for this is the fact that the material first passes a cultural, economic and political qualifications rather than humanist that would be much more accurate. For example, a huge article was devoted to Belgian atrocities in Congo when more than five million people were brutally killed in 1998, On 'Time' magazine for June 5; However, this article did not had success and was virtually ignored by the general public. Moreover, the king of Belgium of that time - Leopold - at ones time was declared a saint by Pope, for his services to humanity, as all of the resources mined in Congo were given to improve the life of Belgians.

So how could this happen? It is not just that 'Time' readers have not much similar with the dead people of the Congo, but also in the fact that all accustomed to fact that people are constantly dying in the 'third world countries'; their life seems to be not as valuable as the life of the American or European. It would seem that the world community is moving away from such barbaric attitudes; however, that was just another one trick. It seems that richer countries are trying to give some help to the third world countries (not forgetting to tell us about this fact), giving them any loans, or interfering in their internal politics. Nevertheless, we used to forget that the wealth and power of the world's economy leaders has often been built thanks to the systematic exploitation of the weaker states and peoples. Thus, what is positioned as a help, in fact, it must be positioned as the return of the debt.

Therefore, thanks to the strong propaganda, which uses increasingly sophisticated covert techniques, is becoming increasingly difficult to determine the real nature of the things that applies not only to the issue of violence, but also in all spheres of our life in general. Nowadays, in the era of late capitalism, all our desires, thoughts, aspirations and dreams are trying to be controlled by media, and using less noticeable leverage which becomes established by increasing the zero mark. After the decline of the ideological tenets of the previous centuries which were often imposed by brute force, media try to control our thoughts more subtle, but often completely unnoticed. It turns out that modern human is originally not just a 'hostages of their own desires', but the hostage imposed by external desires which increases the number of steps on the path to nirvana at least for one more. After all, if all the people are freed from their desires, on what foundation capitalism will be held?

2.5 INCREASED TERRORISM

Terrorism in our time also takes the form of a global problem, especially in the presence of terrorists in deadly drugs or weapons capable of destroying a huge amount of any innocent people. Terrorism is a phenomenon; a form of crime aimed directly against the person, threatening his life, and thereby seeks to achieve its objectives. Terrorism is absolutely unacceptable from the point of view of humanity, and from the point of view of the law is a grave crime.

Terrorism in our time additionally expects the character of a worldwide issue. Particularly within the sight of terrorists in lethal medications or weapons equipped for wrecking a tremendous measure of any guiltless individuals. Terrorism is a type of wrongdoing pointed specifically against the individual and debilitating his life and in this way tries to accomplish its targets. Terrorism is completely unsatisfactory from the perspective of humankind, and from the perspective of the law is a grave wrongdoing.

Terrorism is to a great degree hard to battle in light of the fact that for this situation at danger the lives of blameless individuals taken prisoner or coerced. There can be no avocation for such acts. Dread leads mankind in the time before the advancement of progress - it is cruel savageness where human life in nothing put. He - the ruthless guideline of the spread of blood retribution which is contradictory with any religion built up, the more - the world. All created religion and society of all unequivocally censure terrorism even thinking of it as absolutely unsuitable.

Be that as it may, after unrestricted judgment of this marvel, it is important to consider its causes. The battle with the results and is ineffectual as treatment of dismissed sicknesses. Just by comprehension the reasons for terrorism and dispense with or choosing they can truly win it. In this association, two sorts of reasons for terrorism can be formally recognized: subjective and objective.

Subjective reasons match with the reasons for wrongdoing as a rule; firstly, it is the longing to get rich. But terrorism chooses to gain the wealth in the most cruel and unsatisfactory way. Because of that, terrorism must be battled by all lawful means. For this situation, the discipline ought to be inescapable and extreme.

Anyway, there is terrorism, which has target reasons, for example, one that does not go for individual enhancement, but rather seek after any political or different destinations in the most contemporary terrorism is a supplier of separatism as the battle for national autonomy, yet inadmissible techniques. We need to perceive that the development of national awareness is definitely tends to state enlistment. Acculturated keep away from this issue is conceivable just by making good conditions for the advancement of the country inside the current no national and multinational state. It is important to make bargains and to look for trade off, and try to take care of the issue, instead of stifling it.

However, the likelihood of such an answer for the issue of terrorism is exacerbated by the way that there is a universal terrorist system, which supplies the terrorists as weapons and assets, and gives data help. Furthermore, rather than organizing a mutualbattle against worldwide terrorism, the modern nations have utilized it as a negotiating advantage in the battle against each other. The products of this strategy betrayed those nations who financed and made this system. Overseen terrorism abruptly got wild, and after the disastrous occasions in September 2001 in the United States, we came to understand that the terrorists have their own specific objectives, and that fear must be battled together.

Another target of terrorism, alongside with the national wars is the uneven financial and social improvement in various areas and nations around the globe. Proceeding with operation of the strategy of neo-expansionism and in an inactive structure, this is the fundamental wellspring of worldwide terrorism today. Encouraging cannot comprehend the eager, ravenous and all around nourished; uneducated and uninformed man is continually endeavoring to take care of their issues through brutality. All around bolstered, but profoundly and ethically undeveloped individual dependably looks to live wealthier and better, and not paying consideration on the neediness or unsettled others. In this manner, the fundamental root of terrorism lays in the financial issues of the contemporary world, in the out of line redistribution of riches, in miserable lack of awareness and zeal of some carelessness and fulfillment of others.

The man, intended to lose hope and not having any lawful and genuine types of presentation to a specific circumstance, alludes to the most straightforward - the vicious choice that trusting along these lines you can accomplish something. This way is not substantial, but rather the absence of adequate good and profound improvement prompts enthusiasm and viciousness.

As terrorism has subjective reasons, and with the goal of terrorism there similarly has no avocation. Because of different reasons, the distinction must be assorted strategies to battle this marvel. No misuse of a man who should not be unpunished, but rather you should take after the way of the disposal of the causes that lead to terrorism. Today universal financial request, evidently, drives mankind into a deadlock, and on the off chance that it needs to survive; it must battle for his change. Arrangements most created nations bear an uncommon obligation here, yet they would prefer not to acknowledge the way that the present day world is reliant; it is difficult to survive alone. Their battle for human rights has a double character, and is targeted at some certain geo-political purposes by that being opposed to human interests.

Thus, terrorism may be seen as the most cruel and dangerous loop of human perversion, which is cause by the whole situation, in which a diseased mankind has driven itself into.

3. A VISION OF HUMAN EXISTENCE FROM BUDDHIST PERSPECTIVE

Buddhism was originated in the sixth century BCE in ancient India, which after that was throughout the Asian continent, such as, Nepal, China, Tibet, Japan, Thailand, Myanmar, Lao, Cambodia, Vietnam, etc. and now it has spread throughout the Western and almost Worldwide.

It should be noted that the concept of 'Buddhism' term was invented by the inhabitants of Europe in the 19th century. It is obvious that they named this religion after its founder. But the numerous followers of the teaching themselves name it only as 'Dharma' which means doctrine or principle, or "Buddhadharma" that can be interpreted as the Buddha's teaching (Melton and Baumann 43). There is an opinion that it is impossible to understand all the wisdom and subtlety cultures of India and China, without knowing the intricacies of Buddhism.

3.1 SAMSARIC CYCLE - HUMAN EXISTENCE

Buddhism is a religious and philosophical doctrine; however, Buddhism doesn't fit neatly into either category of religion or philosophy. When people asked Buddha what he was teaching, he said he teaches "the way things are." He said, do not believe his teachings by your faith, but instead you should examine for yourself to see if they are true or not.

As Buddha Shakyamuni claimed, his teaching is a way to self-improvement and self-knowledge. Also Buddhism is a religion in which almost nothing is said about the existence of a higher intelligence - God/Brahmā, as well as the existence of an immortal human soul. The paragraph of Tevijja suttra following was the dialogue between the Buddha and Brahman Vasettha:

'…Well then, Vaseṭṭha, what about the early sages of those Brahmins learned in the Three Vedas, the makers of the mantras, the expounders of the mantras, whose ancient verses are chanted, pronounced and collected by the Brahmins of today, and sung and spoken about - such as Atthaka, Vāmaka, Vāmadeva, Vessāmitta, Yamataggi, Angirasa, Bhāradvāja, Vāsettha, Kassapa, Bhagu did they ever say: "We know and see when, how and where Brahmā appears"?' 'No, Reverend Gotama.'

'So, Vāseṭṭha, not one of these Brahmins learned in the Three Vedas has seen Brahmā face to face, nor has one of their teachers, or teacher's teachers, nor even the ancestor seven generations back of one of their teachers. Nor could any of the early sages say: "We know and see when, how and where Brahmā appears." So what these Brahmins learned in the Three Vedas are saying is: "We teach this path to union with Brahmā that we do not know or see, this is the only straight path…leading to union with Brahmā." What do you think, Vāseṭṭha? Such being the case, does not what these Brahmins declare turn out to be ill-founded?' 'Yes indeed, Reverend Gotama.'

'Well, Vāseṭṭha, when these Brahmins learned in the Three Vedas teach a path that they do not know or see, saying: "This is the only straight path …", this cannot possibly be right. Just as a file of blind men go on, clinging to each other, and the first one sees nothing, the middle one sees nothing, and the last one sees nothing, so it is with the talk of these Brahmins learned in the Three Vedas: the first one sees nothing, the middle one sees nothing, the last one sees nothing. The talk of these Brahmins learned in the Three Vedas turns out to be laughable, mere words, empty and vain.

'Then, Vāseṭṭha, it is like this: not one of these Brahmins ... has seen Brahmā face to face, nor has one of their teachers ...' 'Yes indeed, Reverend Gotama.'

'That is right, Vāseṭṭha. When these Brahmins learned in the Three Vedas teach a path that they do not know and see, this cannot possibly be right..."[1] Thus through this teaching, the Buddha wanted to remind Buddhists having a clearly attitude about the vision of the meaning of life in present to which they need to follow.

However, in Buddhist theory, the human existence is filled with suffering. Suffering is a consequence of the emergence of human desires. According to the opinion of majority of Buddhists, it is freedom from suffering which is a sense of human existence. The Assu Sutta of Pali Canon provides a great explanation of our existence in Saṃsāra: "From an inconstruable (sic) beginning come transmigration. A beginning point is not evident, though beings hindered by ignorance and fettered by craving are transmigrating & wandering on. What do you think, monks: Which is greater, the tears you have shed while transmigrating & wandering this long, long time - crying & weeping from being joined with what is displeasing, being separated from what is pleasing - or the water in the four great oceans?

"As we understand the Dhamma taught to us by the Blessed One, this is the greater: the tears we have shed while transmigrating & wandering this long, long time - crying & weeping from being joined with what is displeasing, being separated from what is pleasing -not the water in the four

---

[1] DN13 Tevijja Sutta: The Threefold Knowledge /the Way to Brahma, translated by T. W. Rhys Davids.

great oceans.

"Excellent, monks, Excellent. It is excellent that you thus understand the Dhamma taught by me.

"This is the greater: the tears you have shed while transmigrating & wandering this long, long time - crying & weeping from being joined with what is displeasing, being separated from what is pleasing - not the water in the four great oceans.

"Long have you (repeatedly) experienced the death of a mother? The tears you have shed over the death of a mother while transmigrating & wandering this long, long time - crying & weeping from being joined with what is displeasing, being separated from what is pleasing - are greater than the water in the four great oceans.

"Long have you (repeatedly) experienced the death of a father... the death of a brother... the death of a sister... the death of a son... the death of a daughter... loss with regard to relatives... loss with regard to wealth... loss with regard to disease. The tears you have shed over loss with regard to disease while transmigrating & wandering this long, long time - crying & weeping from being joined with what is displeasing, being separated from what is pleasing - are greater than the water in the four great oceans. "Why is that? From an inconstruable beginning comes transmigration. A beginning point is not evident, though beings hindered by ignorance and fettered by craving are transmigrating & wandering on. Long have you thus experienced stress, experienced pain, experienced loss, swelling the cemeteries - enough to become disenchanted with all fabricated things, enough to become dispassionate, enough to be released."[1]

---

[1] SN. Assu Sutta: Tears/translated from the Pali by Thanissaro Bhikkhu.

According the teachings above, we can see that samsara means suffering - the endless suffering, and unlimited wandering that Buddhism is keep on rubbing up and down in circles of the six realms: Gods (devas), human (manusya), demi-gods (asuras), hell (naraka), ghosts (petas) and animals (tiryag). And the Buddha was the first to capture the confidence of reincarnation and figure out how to end it. He taught that the only way to end our suffering journey of rebirth is enlightenment. The only one who can stop the samsara cycles of suffering is the person who was crossing his path, and deeply understood his pains.

The basis of the Buddha's teaching concerning human existence and methods to get rid of being sufferings from samsara can be found in the first Dharma which is called the Four Noble Truths. "The Four Noble Truths ('catvāri āryasatyāni' from Sanskrit) represent formulations fully comparable to the formulations of a doctor who diagnoses a patient and prescribes him or her treatment."[1] This metaphor is not accidental because the Buddha actually saw himself as a doctor of living beings - called to heal them from the suffering of samsara and prescribe treatment and leading to recovery, which is nirvana.

And indeed, the first truth ('The Noble Truth of Suffering') is a statement of the disease and sufering; the second truth ('The Noble Truth of the cause of suffering') indicates the cause of the disease (what in modern medicine is referred to as the etiology and pathogenesis); the third truth ('The Noble Truth of the cessation of suffering') is a forecast indication of the possibility of healing; and, finally, the fourth truth (The Noble Truth of the Way) is a course of treatment prescribed to a patient. Thus, from beginning of its existence, Buddhism

---

[1] The Four Noble Truths By Bhikkhu Bodhi.

was conceived as a kind of project of a conversion from being a suffering and ontologically unfortunate person to being free and perfect creature.

Let us consider the Four Noble Truths in detail. So what is the Noble truth of Suffering, and what is suffering (dukkha) in context of Buddhism? According to Francis Story, the Buddha himself formulated the First Noble Truth in a following way: "What, Bhikkhus, is the Noble Truth of Suffering? Birth is suffering; decay is suffering; death is suffering; sorrow, lamentation, pain, grief and despair are suffering. To be separated from the pleasant is suffering; to be in contact with the unpleasant is also suffering. In short, the five aggregates of Existence connected with attachment are all suffering"[1] (What are those 'five aggregates' (pañcaskandhī) will be discussed later in this chapter).

Buddhism, in a much greater extent and vision than other religions, emphasizes the connection of life with suffering. Moreover; in Buddhism, suffering is a fundamental characteristic of being as such. This suffering is not the result of a fall into sin and the loss of the original paradise. Like being itself, suffering invariably accompanies every manifestation of life. Of course, the Buddhists did not deny the fact that in life there are good moments, associated with pleasure, but by itself this pleasure (sukha) is not the opposite of suffering, but is included in suffering, being its aspect.

The point is no mundane states of mind that has the ability to completely satisfy for us. We are in constant dissatisfaction, a constant frustration. We can experience a strong physical or even spiritual (for instance, aesthetic) pleasure and we can even cry out: Stop a moment! But the

---

[1] Francis Story, 'The Foundations of Buddhist Philosophy'

moment does not stop, the pleasure ends, and we suffer because it ended and we seek to re-experience it, but in vain, and we suffer even more. Or, on the contrary: we are committed to something as perhaps devoting our entire life to this. And now we have reached the goal, but we comprehend a bitter disappointment: the fruit was not as sweet as we imagined, and life loses its meaning, because the goal is achieved, and there is nothing more to seek for. And finally, all of us are waiting for death, which makes all of our fun and enjoyment finite and transient.

In other words, suffering is born from the desire, and the endless desire comes from misconceptions about 'me'while going for it that we cannot define clear about how it is.

In "Dukkha, The Fear of Life", Peter Duggan has written about sufferings he clearly recognized as following:

"The Buddha called it Dukkha
That deep presiding feeling
That when you take a real, good look
Its truth you'll be revealing
John Sherman calls it 'Fear of Life'
But the words they mean the same
There's an angst that lives in all of us
It's part of the human game

So everyone is running
They just don't want to know
They'll search for any pleasure
They're seeking that warm glow
That hides behind the minds dull din
Though few folk - see it there
Till they discover one fine day
That joy is everywhere

They'll go and watch the races
Get involved in some grand sport
Get drunk or go and take some drug
To anything they'll resort
They'll laugh a lot; pretend they're happy
Yet look into their eyes
Then you'll know they're playing games
Not many folk are wise

Within us lies the answer
It's always there to see
There's just one thing that one can do
Look in and find the 'me'
As we question each new day
Who is it that is real?
Then the joy will bubble up
So wonderful you'll feel"

Furthermore, not only do we suffer (in the sense of active tormenting), but we always find ourselves in a situation of a passive enduring. It seems that man himself is an architect of his own happiness, but in reality being enmeshed in a tangle of cause and effect relationships and connections; he is not really forges, but he is himself being under the hammer of causality on the anvil of effects.

Speaking of suffering, Buddhism is not limited by human destiny; animals also suffer. Everywhere in nature, the life of one species is dependent on another species, everywhere the life of one being is bought at the cost of another, and everywhere reigns struggle for survival. Sufferings of the inhabitants of the hells are untold, and prets (hungry ghosts) are suffering from never satisfied drives. Even deities (Vedic Brahma, Indra, Varuna and other gods) also suffer. They have to fight with the demons, Asuras, and they are guided by the fear of death because they also are born and die even though their life span is huge. In short, "there is no form of life, which would not be a subject of suffering. Suffering is absolute, and pleasure is relative."[1]

Sometimes we lost what we concern, we are separated from those we love, and our bodies change as we are old, we feel helpless or vulnerable, or our life just seems unfortunate. These are all aspects of suffering - one of the main teachings of the Buddha. Dukkha is suffering, discontent, dissatisfaction, changing...

Dukkha mentions experience sometimes it is conscious, sometimes not consciously-depth fact that everything is impermanent, ungraspable, and not really knowable. On some level, we all understand this. All the things we have, we know we do not really have. All that we see, then we are completely invisible. This is the nature of things, but we think the opposite. We think that we can know, and have our lives our love, our identity, and even our property even though we cannot. The gap between reality and the basic approach to the life of man is suffering - an experience of fundamental anxiety or frustration.

According to Buddha's teaching, we live are trapped in the cycle of reincarnation exists. In the cycle, we wander aimlessly and experience unbearable suffering-day and night, year after year, life after life, because we are grasping the desires to be the self. To heal this sick state of mind, first we have to find the cause of it, and then we apply the methods to cultivate body and mind to restore the original health which is enlightenment. Here is a statement of the disease; here is the diagnosis of a Buddhist physician. But what is the cause of the disease?

---

[1] The Four Noble Truths - By Bhikkhu Bodhi.

3.2 KARMA AND THE 'WHEEL OF LIFE'

The Second Noble Truth is the truth about the cause of suffering. This cause is appetence, desire, attachment to life in the broadest sense, or the will to live. This attraction is understood in Buddhism as widely as possible because this concept includes also abhorrence as the flip side of the drive - drive with the opposite sign. At the heart of life there is a desire for a pleasant and aversion to unpleasant, expressed in the appropriate reactions and motivations, based on a fundamental misconception or ignorance (avidyā), and expressed in the lack of understanding of the fact that the essence of life is suffering. Attraction gives rise to suffering: "if there were no instincts and thirst for life, then there would be no suffering. The whole nature is permeated by this thirst."[1] This thirst seems to be the core of life of every living being, and this life is governed by the law of karma.

The law of karma is the doctrinal core of Buddhism as well as the cause of all the happiness and unhappiness of beings. The word 'karma' can be translated as 'work' or 'action', and by no means as 'destiny' or 'fate' as it is sometimes thought. In Vedic times under karma was understood not any action, but only ritually significant action (for example, the commission of any rite), which gives the desired result, or 'fruit' (phala). Gradually the importance of this concept has expanded and it has come to mean any act, or act in the broadest sense of the word: the physical act (action, deed), the verbal act (word, sentence), and the mental and volitional act (thought, intention, desire).

The following dialogue between Buddhism and Rahula following helping us to understand about 'Karma' meaning in the Buddha time:

---

[1] Ibid...

The Buddha: "What do you think, Rahula: What is a mirror for?"

Rahula: "For reflection, sir."

The Buddha: "In the same way, Rahula, bodily acts, verbal acts, and mental acts are to be done with repeated reflection."[1]

Thus, karma is an action, which necessarily has a consequence or result. The collection of all acts performed in life, or rather, the total energy of these actions also brings its fruit: it determines the need for the next birth - a new life - the nature of which is determined by karma (that is, the nature of the acts) of the deceased.

Accordingly, karma may be good or not good which is leading to good or bad forms of birth. Actually, karma determines in the new birth what philosophers-existentialists call 'abandonment': a country in which a man is to be born (if acquired is the human form of birth), a family of birth, sex and other genetic characteristics (for example, congenital disease), the basic character traits, psychological tendencies, and so on. In this life, a person again commits actions leading him to a new birth, and so on and so forth. This cycle of births-deaths in religions of India (not only in Buddhism) is called samsara (a cycle, circulation) - the main characteristic of which is suffering resulting from the instincts and desires. Therefore, all the religions of India (Buddhism, Hinduism, Jainism and even partly Sikhism) aim to liberation; that is the exit from the cycle of samsara and the attainment of freedom from suffering and passive suffering to which any living creature is doomed by their samsaric existence.[2]

---

[1] Ibid...

[2] Melton and Baumann, 'Religions of the World: A Comprehensive Encyclopedia of Beliefs...'

Samsara is beginningless, which means that none of the creatures had an absolutely first life, they are in samsara eternally. Consequently, samsaric existence is fraught with repeatable situations and roles in painful monotony cyclic reproducibility of the same content. Buddhism is completely alien to the idea of evolution the transition from life to life forms through the will of a Creator; in Indian religions they are not a ladder of improvement and ascent to the Absolute, but the painful circulation and the transition from one form of suffering to another. Therefore, if a person of a materialistic, or simply non-religious Western education can find something attractive in the idea of reincarnation, for Indian thinkers they are associated with a sense of lack of freedom and with painful enslavement, and triggering the need for the release of this whirlwind.

The doctrine of karma and samsara emerged in the pre-Buddhist period within the later Vedic Brahmanism (apparently, not later VIII - VII centuries BCE), but it was Buddhism that elaborated it, articulated clearly and made a forming part of its teaching, and then in final form shared it to Hinduism. However, there are some differences between the Buddhist and Hindu understanding of karma. Thus, it is believed in theistic Hinduism that God determines the effects of karma in dispensing retribution for those or other actions. But Buddhism is not a theistic doctrine, so there is no place for the concept of God and; therefore, karma refers to the Buddhists, not as some kind of retaliation or retribution from God or gods, and as absolutely objective basic law of existence, so just as inevitable as the laws of nature and acting as automatically and impersonally (Guruge). Essentially, the law of karma is simply the result of transferring the idea of the universality of the cause-effect relations in the area of ethics, morality and psychology.

Apart from the human, Buddhism recognizes five other possible forms of existence: birth as a deity (deva), militant titanium (asura) - these two forms of birth as well as human are considered 'happy', and forms of animal, hungry spirit (prets) and inhabitant of hell - unhappy forms of birth. Probably, it is necessary to repeat that any idea of spiritual evolution is not included in this scheme: after death as a deity you can be born again as a person, then may be going to hell, then be born as animal, and then again as a man, then again to go to hell, and so on. It should be noted that only a man (according to some Buddhist thinkers - also deities and asuras) is able to generate karma and thus be responsible for his actions; the other living creatures only reap the benefits of good or bad deeds done by them in the previous human births. Therefore, for example, animals suffer in some way during their lifetime innocently, because the one who are responsible for their karmic suffering is their human precursor.[1]

It is constantly emphasized in Buddhist texts that the human form of birth is particularly favorable: only a human occupies a middle position between the living beings; he is not so immersed in a false bliss, like the gods, but he is also not so exhausted as the inhabitants of the hells. In addition, a man, unlike animals, is endowed with a well-developed intellect. And this midline, central position gives a human being a unique opportunity: only man is capable of gaining liberation from the cycle of samsara and only human is able to get out of the wheel of births and deaths and attain eternal blissful rest in nirvana.[2]

Buddhist texts constantly say that the human body is a rare jewel and finding it is a great happiness, for only a

---

[1] Karma and Rebirth: A Cross Cultural Study/Walter 32

[2] Ibid...

person is able to attain liberation, and therefore it would be most unwise to miss this unique opportunity. Tsongkhapa, a famous Tibetan religious reformer of XIV - XV centuries, compares the probability of acquiring the human body according to Buddhist thought as same as a turtle floating in the world's oceans depths for thousands of years, suddently emerging on the surface, and immediately its head hits in a hole of the only wooden circle which someone thrown into the ocean.[1] Like that, the best thing a human being can meet as Dharma, as Buddhism teaches, so the one can have the opportunity to practice on the path of liberation whether of himself (as taught in Hinayana tradition) or of all living beings (in accordance with the teachings of the Mahayana).

The doctrine of karma as a causal relationship, it means correlated development process in the theory called Pratītyasamutpāda (cause-dependant origination). This theory is extremely important, because later (especially in the framework of the philosophical school Madhyamaka), it essentially became a fundamental methodological principle of Buddhist thought.

The following texts help us more understanding the causal relationship of action in Buddha's teachings:

"There are beings who conduct themselves in a bad way in body ... in speech ... and in mind. But when they often reflect on that fact, which bad conduct in body, speech, and mind will either be entirely abandoned or grow weaker...

"A disciple of the noble ones considers this: 'I am not the only one who is owner of my actions, heir to my actions, born of my actions, related through my actions, and have my actions as my arbitrator; who -- whatever I do, for good or for evil, to that will I fall heir. To the extent that there are

---

[1] Tsongkhapa and Sparham 23

beings - past and future, passing away and re-arising -- all beings are the owner of their actions, heir to their actions, born of their actions, related through their actions, and live dependent on their actions. Whatever they do, for good or for evil, to that will they fall heir.'

When he/she often reflects on this, and the [factors of the] path take birth. He/she sticks with that path, develops it, and cultivates it. As he/she sticks with that path, develops it and cultivates it, the fetters are abandoned, the obsessions destroyed."[1]

Also, if we know how it functions we will not continue to suffer its consequences:

"Kamma should be known. The cause by which kamma comes into play should be known. The diversity in kamma should be known. The result of kamma should be known. The cessation of kamma should be known. The path of practice for the cessation of kamma should be known," thus it has been said.

In reference to what was it said? Intention, I tell you, is kamma. Intending, one does kamma by way of body, speech, and intellect.

What is the agent by which karma creates consequences including further karma?

"And what is the cause by which kamma comes into play? Contact is the cause by which kamma comes into play.

Are there any beings exempt from karmic consequences?

"And what is the diversity in kamma? There is kamma to be experienced in hell, kamma to be experienced in the realm of common animals, kamma to be experienced in the realm of the hungry shades, kamma to be experienced in the human

---

[1] Anguttara Nikaya V.57, Upajjhatthana Sutta/Subjects for Contemplation

world, kamma to be experienced in the world of the devas. This is called the diversity in kamma."

What are the consequences of karma? More karma:

"And what is the result of kamma? The result of kamma is of three sorts, I tell you: that which arises right here and now, that which arises later [in this lifetime], and that which arises following that. This is called the result of kamma.

How can this vicious circle be broken?

"And what is the cessation of kamma? From the cessation of contact is the cessation of kamma; and just this noble eightfold path -- right view, right resolve, right speech, right action, right livelihood, right effort, right mindfulness, right concentration -- is the path of practice leading to the cessation of kamma.

"Now when a disciple of the noble ones discerns kamma in this way, the cause by which kamma comes into play in this way, the diversity of kamma in this way, the result of kamma in this way, the cessation of kamma in this way, and the path of practice leading to the cessation of kamma in this way, then he discerns this penetrative holy life as the cessation of kamma.

Kamma should be known. The cause by which kamma comes into play... The diversity in kamma... The result of kamma... The cessation of kamma... The path of practice for the cessation of kamma should be known.' Thus it has been said, and in reference to this was it said."[1]

Usually, for simplicity and for didactic purposes in The Second Noble Truth, this principle of karmic cause and effect is illustrated in the Buddhist texts (its classic description is contained in the 'Mahavagga', the text of the Pali Tipitaka)

---

[1] Anguttara Nikaya VI.63, Nibbedhika Sutta/Penetrative

as an example of human life, even though, in accordance with the general principles of the Buddhist teachings it can be applied to any element of existence, which appears and disappears every moment of life by Dependent Origination as well as to the whole cosmic cycle. In its description we will follow the classic tradition to see more clearly. The chain of cause and dependent origination consists of twelve units (nidānas), and in principle, no matter how nidānas start the process, since the presence of any of them causes all the others. However, the narration logic requires a certain order, which will be observed here:

I. Previous life (or, more exactly, the gap between death and new birth, antarbhāva)

1. Avidyā (ignorance): Ignorance (in the sense of misunderstanding and misfeeling) of Four Noble Truths, confusion about your own nature and the nature of existence as it is, results in the presence of...

2. Saṃskāra: uniform personality (forming factors, motivation, basic subconscious desires and impulses), involving the decease to a new experience of life, a new birth. Intermediate existence comes to an end, and there is a conception in operating of a new life.

II. This life.

3. Vijñāna (consciousness): The presence of samskāras causes the appearance of consciousness or distinction results to the inside and outside of phenomenon.

4. Nama-rupa (Name and form): They are psychophysical characteristics of human beings. On the basis of these mental and physical structures are formed.

5. Saḍāyatana (six sense bases): Six organs or abilities of sensory perception: 1. Eye and Vision 2. Ear and Hearing 3. Nose and Olfaction 4. Tongue and Taste 5.

Skin and Touch 6. Mind and Thought. That is the sixth "internal" and "external" sense bases are: mind, and, thought (along with memory and emotion).

6. Sparśa (contact): the contact of sense-perception with objects.

7. Vedanā (sensation): feeling of pleasant, unpleasant or neutral; the sense of pleasant and desire to experience it again, give rise to...

8. Tṛṣṇā (craving): which means 'thirst', as the craving or desire to hold onto pleasurable experiences...

9. Upādāna (attachment): that means grasping or clinging; it makes "fuel, material cause, substrate that is the source and means for keeping an active process energized.

10. (Bhava) (becoming): It means being, worldly existence, birth, origin...

III. Next life.

11. Jāti (birth): A new birth; it is the characteristic of whatever is formed

12. Jarā-maraṇa (aging, decay and death): the inevitable decay and death-related suffering of all beings prior to their rebirth within Saṃsāra (cyclic existence).

This was a brief and concise listing of links in the chain of causal relationships. Its main point is that all the stages of existence are caused; this cause is purely immanent in nature and leaving no room for the hidden mysterious transcendent cause (God, fate, etc.). At the same time a living being (not only a human being), one is drawn by their subconscious impulses and drives; the nature of beings as slaves for relentless conditioning in ignorance rather positively to realize it; they just doomed passive suffering position.

In Tibetan Tankas (religious paintings, icons), this doctrine obtains visual embodiment; the Tankas connect with the doctrine of karma and forms of births. Such pictures are called bhava-cakra ('wheel of life') and represent the following: There are three concentric circles. In the central (very small) circle, three animals are imaged: a pig, a snake and a rooster. They seem to grasp the tail of each other and set off to run in a circle (like a squirrel in a wheel) in setting the whole wheel of life into motion. Images of animals symbolize accordingly: ignorance (moha), desire (raga) and aversion (dvesha) - three basic affects (klesha), which form the fundament of samsaric existence.

External to this circle, there is relatively large circle divided into five sectors corresponding to the five worlds of births of living creatures (usually the gods and the titans are portrayed in the same sector). It contains scenes of life of each creature type.

Finally, the last narrow circle that is forming some kind at a rim of a wheel is divided into twelve segments corresponding to twelve nidānas. For example, ignorance is symbolized by the image of a man who has got an arrow in his eye; impulses (saṃskāra) - symbolized by the figure of a potter who is clinging pots on his potter's wheel; the consciousness (vijñāna) - by a monkey that is jumping from branch to branch (consciousness is unstable and tends to jump from one object to another); the name and shape (nama-rupa) - by two people sailing in the same boat; the six bases of perception (saḍāyatana) - by the house with six windows, is a contact of the senses with their objects (sparśa) by a copulating couple, and so on.[1]

Overall of 'wheel of life' is gripped in a god's paws, as if he was embracing it - a scary monster who symbolizes the

---

[1] The Buddhist Wheel of Life - Dharmapala Thangka Centre

suffering as the main feature of samsaric existence. Beyond the wheel in the upper corner of the picture there is usually Buddha (or a monk) depicted that is pointing his finger at the glowing circle around it - which is a symbol of nirvana, a state free from suffering, in its turn, including what is emphasized to the Third Noble Truth.

3.3 NIRVANA AS LIBERATION

The Third Noble Truth is the truth of the cessation of suffering which is nirvana. As a doctor who gives a favorable prognosis to a patient, the Buddha states that despite the fact that suffering pervades all levels of samsaric existence; there is a state in which there is no suffering and that this condition is achievable: It is nirvana.

The word 'nirvana' goes back to the Sanskrit root nirvāṇa; it means 'blown out', and refers to the extinguishing of the fires of greed, hatred and delusion; 'nir' meaning fading, or attenuation (for example, the attenuation of the lamp or cessation of rough seas). On this basis, the XIX century researchers of Buddhism often built their theory of nirvana as the complete cessation of life - a kind of complete dying, so after that Buddhism was accused in total pessimism. However, Buddhist texts indicate quite clearly that it is not the being that dies or fades. One of the most common images that are used in the text to illustrate the idea of nirvana are such: just as an icon lamp ceases to light, running out of the oil that fuels the fire, or just like a surface of the sea stops worrying when the wind stops, so in the same way all the suffering stops when all the affects which feed the suffering run out. Thus, suffering, passion, affection and obscuration are attenuated, and not being itself. With the disappearance of the causes of suffering, suffering itself disappears.

Getting rid of suffering is possible in only one way, and for that it is necessary to reach a state called enlightenment or nirvana (Pali: 'nibbana'). Nirvana is a state of supreme bliss in which a person does not feel any kind of need for something. In state of Nirvana, he does not feel desire, suffering and attachments, and he is not affected by the events of life.

Nirvana actually has a very simple meaning; Nirvana literally means "cool" or "to extinguish", and different from what most people usually thinking such as heavenly realm where you want to enjoy the things you like.

Nirvana literally is a state where suffering has been 'extinguished'. Or said another way, the flames of desire have been cooled as greed, such as hatred and delusion would no longer control you. In short, it is a state of the ultimate freedom - freedom from sorrow, but also freedom from happiness.

In addition, some teachings in Buddhism call nirvana the exit from another state of being - samsara (Billington 54 - 60). Samsara is a series of rebirths, so this is also the state in which at the moment we all are. Being in samsara, a person suffers and is reborn from one body to another. At the same time, the results of his past actions affect the course of his present and later life, which is called karma. Naturally, good actions return to the person as good and bad actions as bad. Buddhism promotes good karma to help people to exit from the painful state of samsara and the transition to a state of transcendental bliss, so nirvana is the main purpose of life for most Buddhists. Nirvana state just occurs due to ongoing work with your own consciousness, as well as to the conduct of a righteous life in the world.

So what is Nirvana? The Buddha himself never gave

a straight answer to this question and tried to keep silent when the question was still asked. Here Buddha happens to be a direct precursor of the famous philosopher of the XX century Ludwig Wittgenstein, who proclaimed, "Whereof one cannot speak, thereof one must be silent."[1] Back in the early Upanishads, Brahmanical texts of philosophical nature, it said that the Absolute (Brahman) can speak only in negative terms (not this, not that), because the Absolute transcends our experience is incomprehensible for thought and inexpressible in words and concepts ("Brahma Upanishad"). Nirvana, which as the Buddha teaches, is not God and is not the impersonal Absolute, and his silence is not apophatic theology. Nirvana is not a substance, but a state, a state of freedom and of a peculiar, impersonal or transpersonal fullness of being. But this state as absolutely transcendent to all our samsaric experiences in which there is nothing like Nirvana:

None of the three worlds (of Desire, Form, and Formlessness) is eternal; all that exists:

It is not happy. What exists has a nature and characteristics.

And all is Void. What is destructible comes and goes,

Apprehensions and illnesses follow upon [one's] steps.

The fears of all the wrongs and evils done,

Age, illness, death and decline cause worry.

All these things do not exist forever.

And they easily break up. Resentment attacks one;

All are lined with illusion, as in the case of the silkworm and the cocoon.

None who has wisdom finds joy in a place like this.

---

[1] Ludwig Wittgenstein, Notebooks 1914-1916 p.398

This carnal body is where suffering forgathers.

All is impure, like unto strains, carbuncles, boils, and other such.

No reason is at bottom. The same applies

Even to the heavenly ones who sit above.

All desires do not last. So I do not cling.

One casts off desires, meditates well,

Attains the wonderful Dharma, and one who definitely

Cuts off 'is' (samsaric existence) can today gain Nirvana.

I pass over to the other shore of "is"

And stand above all sorrows.

Thus I harvest this superb Bliss."[1]

That is why even psychologically it is more correct to say nothing of nirvana than to compare it to something known to us, otherwise we will immediately construct our own nirvana, create a mental image of nirvana, then improper understanding of it. Then we will adhere to this view in such a way making nirvana as our object of affection and this causes source of suffering. Because of that, Buddha limited himself with the most common characteristics of nirvana, such as a state free from suffering, or as the ultimate happiness (nibbanam paramam sukham). Afterwards Buddhists have developed many different concepts of nirvana, but the recognition of its non-semiotic nature will remain in Buddhism forever (Gomez 600 - 606).

But how to achieve liberation, nirvana? This is indicated by the Fourth Noble Truth, the truth of the path (marga) leading to the cessation of suffering, which is the Noble Eightfold Path (Ariya-Ashtanga Marga) that we will discuss in details in Chapter 6.

---

[1] Sarao, The Mahayana Mahaparinirvana Sutra (大般涅槃經) p. 18-19

3.4 *ANATTA (selflessness)* - *ELEMENTS OF SKANDHAS AND DHARMAS*

Therefore, we have concluded our analysis of the Four Noble Truths of Buddhism, and proceed to such an important Buddhist doctrine of the doctrine of non-existence of an individual substantial simple and eternal 'self', or plainly soul (Atman) which in Sanskrit is usually called anatmavada. This Buddhist doctrine distinguishes Buddhism from the majority of the non-Indic religions as well as other Indian religions (Hinduism, Jainism) which recognize the doctrine of 'self' (Atman) and a soul (jiva).[1]

"You, monks, should not thus cultivate the notion (samjna) of impermanence, suffering and non-Self, the notion of impurity and so forth, deeming them to be the true meaning [of the Dharma], as those people [searching in a pool for a radiant gem but foolishly grabbing hold of useless pebbles, mistaken for priceless treasure] did, each thinking that bits of brick, stones, grass and gravel were the jewel. You should train yourselves well in efficacious means. In every situation, constantly meditate upon [bhavana] the idea [samjna] of the Self, the idea of the Eternal, Bliss, and the Pure ... Those who, desirous of attaining Reality [tattva], meditatatively cultivate these ideas, namely, the ideas of the Self [atman], the Eternal, Bliss, and the Pure, will skillfully bring forth the jewel, just like that wise person [who obtained the genuine, priceless gem, rather than worthless detritus misperceived as the real thing.]"[2]

"... one who knows himself (atmanam) as nondual, he wisely knows both Buddha and Dharma. And why? He develops a personality (atmabhava) which consists of all

---

[1] Ibid...

[2] The Buddha, Chapter Three, "Grief", The Mahayana Mahaparinirvana Sutra

dharmas [phenomena] for all dharmas are fixed on the self in their own-being (atma-svabhava-niyata). One who wisely knows the nondual dharma, wisely knows also the Buddhadharmas. From the comprehension of the nondual dharma follows the comprehension of the Buddhadharmas and from the comprehension of the self, the comprehension of everything that belongs to the triple world. 'The comprehension of self', that is the Beyond of all dharmas ..."[1]

"The Tathagata also teaches, for the sake of all beings, that there is, in truth, the Self in all phenomena"[2]

Why Buddhism denies the existence of an eternal 'self'? In answering this question, we are immediately confronted with the difference between from the Indian and European thinking. As it is well known, Kant considered the immortality of the soul to be one of the postulates of morality (Kant). Buddhism, on the other hand, argues that a sense of 'self' and the attachment to this self is the source of all other affections, passions and instincts - all of which forms the 'clesha', the darkened affectivity that spans a living being into the quagmire of samsaric existence.

Which 'self' exactly is denied by Buddhists? Buddhism does not say anything about the Atman, described in the Upanishads, which is the absolute subject, or certain higher transpersonal Self - same for all beings and eventually identical to the Absolute (Brahman). This Atman is neither accepted nor denied by Buddhism. There is nothing about it at least in early texts. It denies specifically the individual 'self' as the essence of the personality, simple and eternal

---

[1] The Buddha in the «perfect insight» scripture, The Questions of Suvikrantavikramin, from Perfect Wisdom: The Short Prajnaparamita Texts, tr. by Edward Conze, BPG, England, 2002.

[2] The Mahaparinirvana Sutra, Chapter Three, translated into English by Kosho Yamamoto, 1973

substance identical to itself. Buddhism does not find it in our experience and views it as an illusory product of mental construction. Thus, basically, Buddhism denies what in the Brahmin and Jain traditions is called jiva (soul) or pudgala (personality).[1]

But if such an entity as a soul does not exist, then what is personality? Buddhists answer that personality is just a name for the groups of psychophysical elements connected in a specific order. In the famous Buddhist philosophical work 'The Questions of King Milinda' (Milinda Pañha), a Buddhist monk Nagasena talks about it with the Greek and Indian King Milinda. The King argues that if Buddhists believe that there is no soul and self, without the elements of human psychophysical structure as well as the complex of all these elements is not a personality (living being), then the king turned his question for the monk again: is there no personality (human) not at all (?) Objecting to the king, Nagasena points at a chariot and starts to ask the king what it is: are wheels a chariot? Or, perhaps, the carcass is the chariot? Or some other details are a chariot? To all these questions, the king gives a negative answer. Then Nagasena asks the king, is a chariot not all of the parts together? Milinda gives a negative answer again, and it gives Nagasena the ability to say that in this case it turns out that there are no chariots at all. Then he clearly explained that chariot is only the name designed to denote the set of all these parts and components. This response enables Nagasena to say that in the same way personality is only a name to represent a unity of the five groups of elements of experience ordered in a particular way.[2]

In Buddhist tradition those groups of elements are called pañcaskandhī, where skandha means a pile, those are:

---

[1] Arshdeep Sarao, The Story of Buddha Sakyamuni

[2] The Questions of King Milinda, translated by T. W. Rhys Davids

- a group of form (rupa) - which is all that we could be attribute to the field of the sensible and material;
- a group of sensation (vedanā) - feeling of pleasant, unpleasant or neutral;
- a group of perception (saṃjñā) - round / square, white / black, etc., as well as the formation of ideas and concepts;
- a group of mental formations (samskāra) - volitions and motivating impulses, this group of elements is responsible for the formation of karma;
- consciousness as such (vijñāna). (Boisvert 669)

The Buddha clearly when a monk asked about the aggregates:

"Whatever form is past, future, or present; internal or external; blatant or subtle; common or sublime; far or near: That is called the form.

"Whatever feeling is past, future, or present; internal or external; blatant or subtle; common or sublime; far or near: That is called the feeling aggregate.

"Whatever perception is past, future, or present; internal or external; blatant or subtle; common or sublime; far or near: That is called the perception aggregate.

"Whatever (mental) fabrications are past, future, or present; internal or external; blatant or subtle; common or sublime; far or near: Those are called the fabrications aggregate.

"Whatever consciousness is past, future, or present; internal or external; blatant or subtle; common or sublime; far or near: That is called the consciousness aggregate.

"These are called the five aggregates.

"And what are the five clinging-aggregates?

"Whatever form - past, future, or present; internal or external; blatant or subtle; common or sublime; far or near - is clingable, offers sustenance, and is accompanied with mental fermentation: That is called the form clinging-aggregate.

"Whatever feeling - past, future, or present; internal or external; blatant or subtle; common or sublime; far or near - is clingable, offers sustenance, and is accompanied with mental fermentation: That is called the feeling clinging-aggregate.

"Whatever perception - past, future, or present; internal or external; blatant or subtle; common or sublime; far or near - is clingable, offers sustenance, and is accompanied with mental fermentation: That is called the perception clinging-aggregate.

"Whatever (mental) fabrications - past, future, or present; internal or external; blatant or subtle; common or sublime; far or near - are clingable, offer sustenance, and are accompanied with mental fermentation: Those are called the fabrications clinging-aggregate.

"Whatever consciousness - past, future, or present; internal or external; blatant or subtle; common or sublime; far or near - is clingable, offers sustenance, and is accompanied with mental fermentation: That is called the consciousness clinging-aggregate.

"They are called the five clinging-aggregates."[1]

It should be brought to attention that the order of the skandhas is not accidental. It reflects the order of the perception of an object and its exploration by a consciousness.

---

[1] Khandha Sutta: Aggregates translated from the Pali by Thanissaro Bhikkhu

In the beginning, there is only a sensual data, then comes a feeling of pleasant or unpleasant which accompanies it, and the formation of a certain image of the perceived object and then forming a processing set on the attraction to apprehension or perception of it. All these processes are accompanied by the participation of consciousness that exists on each level.

The important nuance in Buddhism is that into the concept of personality is also included an object field perceived by a living being. There is no singular man and singular object that he perceives; there is a kind of a field of experience where a man perceives an object. Here the object is no longer an external object, staying out of the person, but a part of a person included in it through the process of perception. This is not an object itself, but the reflection already perceived by a man and which, therefore, became a part of his inner world, a part of a human personality.[1] This is not the world in which we live; this is the world we are living through.

Although Buddhism denies a singular simple soul, it still recognizes some substances as such as bricks from which personality is constituted. Those bricks are five skandhas; however, skandhas are not substances; they are videlicet groups of elements, and their allocation is rather conditional and formal. What is real, it is the elements of the skandhas, which are called dharmas. The teaching about dharmas (Abhidharma) is one of the most complex and also the central themes of Buddhist philosophy.

Dharma is an indivisible element of our psychophysical experience, or it is an elementary psychophysical condition. Is it possible to consider dharma a substance? It is not, for two reasons. Firstly, according to the Indian understanding of the substance and substantiality, for example, Brahmanical

---

[1] Mathieu Boisvert, The Five Aggregates p.669-700

school Nyaya, one of the main ideological opponents of Buddhism which adhered to the substance is always the carrier of the plurality of qualities that are associated with it in different connections while in Buddhism each dharma carries only one quality of its own. Secondly, the Indian substancialists asserted the principle of difference between the carrier (substance) and the carried (accidental, qualities) that was expressed in the formula 'dharma - dharmin bheda' where dharma is a quality that is carried, and dharmin is its substantial carrier. Buddhism claims that dharma and dharmin are identical; the carrier and the carried by them are the same quality. There is also a third fundamental difference: substance of Brahmins, as a rule, is eternal, while, in Buddhism, dharmas are instantaneous.

Another essential thing about dharmas is that in majority of Buddhist schools dharmas are considered, on the one hand, as dravya, which means the elements endowed with ontological status, real elements, and, on the other hand, as prajnapti, that is as just conceivable, conventional, or units of language describing the experience. It means that our experience is constituted by dharmas, but dharmas themselves are also described in terms of dharmas. Here it is possible to bring a somewhat rough parallel: our speech consists of words, but the words we describe in words as well.

This specific of understanding the dharmas by Buddhists brought them close to the resolution of the so-called paradox of mental processes, which the European psychology began to be realize only in the XX century: we always describe consciousness not in the immanent terms (terms, reflecting their own inherent properties), but in terms of the outside world or another consciousness. By introducing the concept of dharma as both ontologically relevant element of consciousness and experience in general and as a language element of a description of consciousness (and experience); the Buddhists, in essence, found a variant of the language of describing consciousness which is immanent to consciousness. This is undeniable contribution from Buddhism to the world philosophy.

Thus, Buddhism looks at personality as merely at a name established to identify a structurally ordered combination of five groups of insubstantial and instant elementary of psychophysical states and dharmas. This is quite a rigorous formulation of the principle of anatmavada ('no-self', 'no-soul'), or more precisely, one of its two aspects - the non-essential personality (pudgala nairatmya).

In Buddhist philosophical literature (Abhidharma), there are various lists and classifications of dharma. For example, school of Sarvastivadins (Vaibhashika) provides a list of seventy-five dharmas, and the list of yogakarins (Vijnanavadins) includes already one hundred dharmas. Firstly, If we talk about the classifications of dharmas, they can be classified in a relation to skandhas aggregates (dharmas related to rupa skandha and vedana skandhas). This five-part list can be reduced to a binary: dharma rupa skandhas and dharmas of all other skandhas (according to the division of constitutions of personality to nāma and rūpa - mental and physical). In this case, the second group of dharmas is named dharma dhatu (dharma element) because dharmas as members of the 'dharma dhatu' are objects of mind (manas), which as we remember from the chain analysis of cause-effect origination, are related by Buddhists to perceptual abilities. Dharmas relating to the saṃskāraskandha are also typically divided into associated with the mental (citta samprayukta) and not associated with mental (citta viprayukta).[1]

---

[1] Willemen, Entrance into the Supreme Doctrine p.219-224

Secondly, dharmas are often divided into sanskrita dharma (included the compositions) and asanskrita dharmas (not included the compositions). The first type is so named empirical dharmas, which are the elements which constitute our samsaric experience - dharmas belonging to the five skandhas of living beings. The second type is over-empirical dharmas, the dharmas that are not related to everyday experience. It is an absolute space or a space of deployment of mental experience (Akasha) and two types of cessation (nirodha, which is suppressing state of functioning of empirical dharmic streams, nirvana): cessation associated with knowledge (pratisamkhya nirodha) and cessation not associated with knowledge (apratsamkhya nirodha). Moreover, dharmas are divided into elapsing with affects (sasrava) and not elapsing with affects (anasrava). First are dharmas which involve in the cycle of samsara; in the process of Buddhist practice they are subjected to a gradual elimination. Also a dharma of 'true path' (marga satya) stands alone: although the path to nirvana, as well as nirvana itself which can be the object of attachment, but this certain attachment does not lead to the accession of affects to this dharma, because they do not find a support in it. But in general, this type of dharmas should be considered karmically bad (akushala). The second type of dharmas, on the contrary, contributes to the acquisition of good (kushala) qualities and promotion on the path to nirvana. The same goes also for those of dharmas that are not included in the compositions.[1]

Dharmas constantly appear and disappear, being replaced by new, but conditioned by previous dharmas arising from the law of cause and dependent origination. These constantly arising and fading non-substrate dharmas

---

[1] Ibid...

in their totality form a stream or a continuum (santana) which empirically are found as a living being. Thus, any creature, including human personality is not understood in Buddhism as unchanging essence (soul, atman), but as a stream of constantly changing elementary psychophysical states. Ontology of Buddhism is the ontology of non-substrate process.

Another essentially important feature of the Buddhist world is closely related to the theory of dharmas. It is the doctrine of momentariness (kshanikavada). Buddhism asserts that samsaric existence is characterized by the following features:

- Everything is impermanent (anitya)

- Everything is suffering (duhkha)

- Everything is deprived of self (anatma)

- Everything is inauspicious (ashubha). (Coseru)

The doctrine of momentariness follows directly from the first thesis of the universality of impermanence. It argues that each dharma (and, respectively, the whole complex of dharmas) exists for only one negligible moment, in the next moment being replaced by a new dharma, and caused by previous one. In this way, we cannot not only enter the same river twice, but there is actually no one who could do something for a second time. In essence, every new moment there is a new one which causally related to the previous one and conditioned by it (Coseru).

In Dhammapada we find the Buddha's words about this impermanence of existence: "There can be, bhikkhu," the Blessed One said. "Here, bhikkhu, someone has the view: 'This is self, this the world; after death I shall be permanent, everlasting, eternal, not subject to change; I shall endure as long as eternity.' He hears the Tathagata or a disciple of the Tathagata teaching the Dhamma for the elimination of all standpoints, decisions, obsessions, adherences, and underlying tendencies, for the stilling of all formations, for the relinquishing of all attachments, for the destruction of craving, for dispassion, for cessation, and for Nibbana. He thinks thus: 'So I shall be annihilated! So I shall perish! So I shall be no more!' Then he sorrows, grieves, and laments; he weeps beating his breast and becomes distraught. That is how there is agitation about what is non-existent internally."[1]

Thus, according to the theory of momentariness, a stream of dharmas that forms a living being is not only a continuum, but is discrete at the same time. If using a modern metaphor, it is best to compare it to a film: it consists of separate frames; however, we do not see when we watch a movie and perceive it as a pure continuum. In this case, the difference between the two adjacent frames is completely insignificant, and they appear to the naked eye as almost identical although the difference is growing and occurs gradually. In this example, each new life is a new episode of a series without beginning, and nirvana is the finale of the movie.

However, here, another question may arise: if there is no soul, then what is reborn and proceeds from life to life? The answer is quite paradoxical: nothing is reborn and nothing proceeds. In contrast to a popular belief, in Buddhism there are no teachings about rebirths or reincarnations from an unchanging soul. A man in Buddhism is not an embodied soul, as in Hinduism. He is a continuous flow of the states - dharmas - a series of shots that are moments.

---

[1] Bhikkhu Nanamoli, and Bhikkhu Bodhi, The Middle Length Discourses of the Buddha p.230

4. BUDDHIST VIEW ON CAUSES OF VIOLENCE, CONFLICT AND WAR, AND THE WAY OF BYPASS

Every society has conflicts of interests and views, both internal and external. Buddhist teachings talk about ways to prevent the emergence of new conflicts and prevent the escalation of those which have already begun. The Buddhists seek to achieve this by explaining to people involved in the conflict on how best to educate their actions, emotions, and understanding of life.

4.1 CONFLICT AND VIOLENCE AS THE ROOTS OF GREED AND HATRED

In Buddhism, violence is considered to be the least intelligent response to the conflict. Violence, physical or verbal, does not create long-term solutions to problems. Those who are responsible for the violence generate heavy karma by their actions, for which they, in the end, have to pay. Victims of violence or their family members seek revenge; thus begins the cycle of violence. The root causes of the conflict remain untreated.

According to Dhammapada, to resolve the root causes of conflict from hatred and anger, the first best ways are forgiveness and compassion for our enemies:

Uncontrolled hatred leads to harm:

Who bears within them enmity:
'He has abused and beaten me,
Defeated me and plundered me,'
Hate is not allayed for them.[1]

---

[1] Translated from Pali by Ven. Weragoda Sarada Maha Thero/DhP3

(Akkocchi maṃ avadhi maṃ
Ajini maṃ ahāsi me
Ye ca taṃ upanayhanti
Veraṃ tesaṃ na sammati.)

Overcoming anger:

Who bears within no enmity
'He has abused and beaten me
Defeated me and plundered me,'
Hate is quite allayed for them. [1]

(Akkocchi maṃ avadhi maṃ
Ajini maṃ ahāsi me
Ye ca taṃ nupanayhanti
Veraṃ tesūpasammati.)

Hated is overcome only by non-hatred:

Never here by enmity
Are those with enmity allayed
They are allayed by amity
This is the timeless Truth.[2]

(Na hi verena verāni
Sammantīdha kudācanaṃ
Averena ca sammanti
Esa dhammo sanantano.)

The Buddha also said that minds can be free from contaminated mental states by taking the most reasonable long-term solutions. Greed, a sense of self-worth and prejudices arising in the minds of the individuals, and being unattended can have enormous consequences for the communities and peoples. The Buddha taught his disciples to constantly look inward to determine how they contribute

---

[1] Ibid...DhP4

[2] Ibid...DhP5

to the emergence of external conflicts with their actions and words, desires and emotions, their beliefs, life values, and theories. He taught the ways of releasing the destructive aspects of the human mind and how to cultivate the constructive aspects. Buddhists learn to identify the causes and conditions of conflict, as well as learn to make efforts in order to be able to resolve the conflict in the best possible way.

Buddhism considers violence, conflict and war, along with all other elements of being to be the result of conditions and causes. In the 'Avatamsaka Sutra' the universe is described as an infinite network which gained its existence from the will of the Bodhisattvas. In each junction of the infinite network there is a polished gem with an infinite number faces fastened perfectly, and each of which reflects all facets of every stone in this network. Because the network being itself, a number of the stones and a number of each face of every stone are endless, then the amount of reflections is also infinite. When every stone in this endless network is in any way changed, the change influences all the other stones in the network (Avatamsaka Sutra/The Flower Garland Sutra). The story of Indra's net poetically explains the mysterious connection that we sometimes witness between seemingly unconnected events.

> "All mistakes that are
> And all the various kinds of evil
> Arise through the force of conditions:
> They do not govern themselves."[1]

In any case, according to the concept of dependent origination, to make violence disappear, we have to destroy the underlying causes of it. From the viewpoint of Buddhism

---

[1] Geshe Kelsang Gyatso, How to Solve Our Human Problems: The Four Noble Truths

there are three categories of conflict and violence: the root causes, the internal causes, and the external causes. External influences are someone's physical or verbal actions against a person that are opposite to the intentions of doing no harm (ahimsa) to this person, or those which prevent someone from obtaining happiness. Although external influences such as physical and verbal harmful deeds or social inequity cause conflicts, Buddhism argues that all that is derived from consciousness of people. Those are emotions such as anger, hate, resentment, contempt, etc. The root causes of violence are, actually, the primary reason of all suffering which is human ignorance (Der-lan Yeh, 94-96). Most of the people are still not aware of the fact that everything is interrelated and all actions derive the results. Most of the people are not aware of the fact that we all are a single living organism.

The cause of the suffering of the people, as explained in Buddhist terms is greed, hatred and delusion. These negative characteristics and the basic evils devastate our inner, and affect outside dangerously which are called the Three Poisons. They are pollutants to cause suffering, which brought physically and mentally diseases for our lives.

The essence of greed is the longing, desire and attachments cause us to want to 'get hold of' things we like. Greed never know satisfaction; it is a companion of hatred, jealousy, disputes leading to big conflicts when we don't achieve what we aspire. The greed's arising is rooted in ignorance-misunderstanding about our ego just temporary conditions...not realizing our true nature, so paving the way for this illusion to another illusion.

These toxins make our life overunning of misery, unhappiness and dissatisfaction. They get us to create awkward decisions which affect our present and the future life and others. They lead us doing immoral actions aimed at self-service to our dishonesty; they create a disordered society being full of conflicts and suspicions. They are the roots not only cause pain and suffering for us but for our loved ones and society. Fortunately, there is a way to eradicate this trio of contaminants by practicing love and compassion- a remedy of wisdom for the best antidote.

Many of us tend to be dominated by one of these toxins. When one of the three poisons to be dominated, other ones are dormant for lacking of conditions for development. For example, if we are governed by anger, we tend to suffer from depression or obsessive about opposing political views - real or imagined enemies, and so would have the negative behavior to life. If we are governed by greed, our behavior is manifested by the desire of what we do not have, being stingy, and lack of compassion for others…Greed inherent in the material things and do not know how to be enough, and just suppose that happier with more possessions. Because of ignorance we don't realize the potential of enlightenment inside us being the true happiness; that is also nature Buddha nature. The unknowing causing insecurity for ourselves; it is also the feeling of weakness, impotence and indifference.

In addition to the domination of greed, states of mind which usually lead to violence and conflict are anger and hatred. Buddhism sees two reasons for hatred and anger: failure to perform what was desired, and sorrowful experiences. When we are unhappy and dissatisfied, we are easily provoked; we are easy to come into a state of anger and hatred. If we are satisfied and happy then something cannot irritate us that easily. Shantideva says that is very important to prevent the occurrence of the unfortunate state of mind that is ready to occur. This sense of unhappiness and is a fuel, a breeding ground for hate and anger. Therefore, it is important to be attentive to our inner world and track those states of mind which are about to appear and make us miserable. It is a condition that is necessary to prevent, so that it does not result in anger and hatred:

Violence always comes from suffering.

"For the sake of satisfying my desires
I have suffered numerous burnings in hell,
But by those actions I fulfilled the purpose
Of neither myself nor others
But now since great meaning will accrue
From harm which is not even (a fraction) of that,
I should indeed by solely joyful
Towards such suffering that dispels the harms of all."[1]

There are also two types of anger known in Buddhism: anger that appears when someone does harm to us, and anger that comes from a sense of dissatisfaction with the success of the enemies. We do not like the fact that someone who reaches success, while we do not. Dalai Lama says, "In Buddhism in general, a lot of attention is paid to our attitudes towards our rivals or enemies. This is because hatred can be the greatest stumbling block to the development of compassion and happiness. If you can learn to develop patience and tolerance towards your enemies, then everything else becomes much easier - your compassion towards all others begins to flow naturally"[2]

"Overcome the angry by non-anger; overcome the wicked by goodness; overcome the miser by generosity; overcome the liar by truth."[3]

However, it is not useful to suppress the anger. At first, the practice of suppression can actually give a short-term effect, but it still; after that it will break and sweep

---

[1] Ibid...

[2] Dalai lama, Shifting Perspective p.178-179

[3] Dhammapada 223

away everything in its path. Much can be gained from the practice of letting go of anger. We need to let the anger go away naturally by itself. Where was the anger a few seconds ago? Let it go back to that place. If we remember how many times we were angry throughout our life, we will see that all coming to a situation of no long time. Feeling of transience of anger has function as an intellectual justification for understanding that everything that comes, goes away. When mindfully working with this practice, you must remain aware of the benefits of patience, and shortcomings of anger what patience leads us to, and what anger leads us to. Over time, in case of a continuous practice, it becomes a habit. We have already clearly understand the experience of anger if it is anger, that it will not lead to anything good and bad, and it is just much wiser to be patient.

> "Unruly beings are as unlimited as space
> They cannot possibly all be overcome
> But if I overcome thoughts of anger alone
> This will be equivalent to vanquishing all foes."[1]

Anger is also rooted from greed and ignorance inside us. Buddhist doctrine teaches us the three poisons linked to social conditions in which we live. For example, greed is reflected to people's poverty and the destruction of the environment. However, it is also the impermanence, change and transition. Greed can be transformed into kindness, or anger can transform into a force to against intolerance, injustice and immorality...

If we are aware of the three toxins and what causes and cure them are, we can achieve great results. Through the practice of good karma and compassion, the hazardous poisons can be transformed into energy gentle, and violent

---

[1] Geshe Kelsang Gyatso, How to Solve Our Human Problems: The Four Noble Truths

conflicts would turn into love and peace, so true happiness would be developed. As we recognize the interrelationship between us with others, coherence and unity of living beings in world, we can excrete the toxins which make our bodies and minds with constant disabilities.

Another special method of discipline which can transform the disputes into harmony and joy in Buddha's teachings we should learn.

In Samagama sutta, The Buddha guided his path to give us having best resolve to the disputes and conflicts in the Sangha community and can apply for our society:

'Aananda, do you see any instance in this Teaching, by me realized and proclaimed where two bhikkhus could dispute, such as in the four establishments of mindfulness, the four right endeavours, the four psychic powers, the five mental faculties, the five powers, the seven enlightenment factors and the eightfold path?' 'Venerable sir, in this Teaching realized and proclaimed by the Blessed One I do not see an instance where two bhikkhus could dispute, such as in the four establishments of mindfulness, the four right endeavours, the four psychic powers, the five mental faculties, the five powers, the seven enlightenment factors and the eightfold path.

Yet those persons who live as though obedient to the Blessed One now, will arouse a dispute on account of the hard livelihood because of the higher code of rules, it will be not for the well being of many and the well being of gods and men.' Ananda, a dispute on the harsh livelihood or the higher code of rules is negligible, if the community has a dispute about the path and method, it will be for the unpleasantness of many, and the unpleasantness of gods and men.'[1]

---

[1] **Sāmagāma Sutta,** Translated from Pali by Bhikkhu Bodhi

Conflict is a process, it is resentment and antagonism prevailing values and uncooperative. Almost any human action it has the ability to look forward to the hope or interfere in other people's plans. Such action would become a conflict; the conflicts in different paths and views could undermine the approach the paths and methods which can bring to many benefits of happiness for many.

Through it, a party trying to eliminate or reduce the other possibility of dependent position is another matter. Though violence often related to the conflict, it can occur without. As Civil disobedience and nonviolent Satyagraha with nonviolent spirit leader - Gandhiji, fought against the ritish imperialism is the best illustration.

Shelly Shah supposes the following characteristics of 4 social conflicts may be noted:

(i) Conflict is a conscious act. That's deliberate opposition.

(ii) Conflict is a individual activity.

(iii) Conflict lacks continuity.

(iv) Conflict is universal.

Also, in Sangha community, there are 6 characteristics of conflicts; the cause of the conflicts are derived from anger and hated, and he lives indulgence; if he recognizes it he can prevent it:

'Aananda, these six are the causes for a dispute. What are the six? When the bhikkhu becomes angry and bears a grudge, he becomes unruly even towards the Teacher, rebels against the Teaching and becomes unruly, rebels against the Community and becomes unruly, does not live complete in the training. Thus he arouses a dispute in the Community, for the unpleasantness of many and the unpleasantness of gods and men. Aananda, if you see this cause for a dispute internally or externally, you should make effort for the dispelling of that cause for a dispute, and for its non arising again.

'Again, Aananda, the bhikkhu is merciless with hypocrisy ...re... jealous and selfish,..re... crafty and fraudulent,...re... is with evil desires and wrong view,...re.. holding fast to worldly matters and not giving up easily. When the bhikkhu holds fast to worldly matters and does not give up easily, he becomes unruly even towards the Teacher, rebels against the Teaching and becomes unruly, rebels against the Community and becomes unruly, does not live complete in the training. Thus he arouses a dispute in the Community, for the unpleasantness of many and the unpleasantness of gods and men. Aananda, if you see this cause for a dispute internally or externally, you should make effort for the dispelling of that cause for a dispute, and for its non arising again. This is dispelling the evil causes of disputes, for their non arising in the future. Aananda, these are the six causes for disputes." [1]

Generally, the conflicts in the Sangha community as well as social community is the big problems; they are the matter of moral beliefs which have no based place only. These bad conflicts are likely tended to results from a clash between the differences of world views of perceptions. However, the conflict was started up from a puzzle person with evil mind to justify for his disengage completely different from conflict to build to a moral order of the social community. In order to address these bad conflicts, the Buddha mentioned four basic laws and seven ways to dispute resolution.

"Aananda, there are four administrations. What are the four? The questions of disputes, questions of censure, questions of misconduct and questions of duties; Aananda,

---

[1] MN. III,Saamagaamasutta.m/At Samagama

there are seven ways to settle all these disputes. Proceedings done in the presence of the accused, appealing to the conscience of the accused, acquittal on grounds of restored sanity, agreement by a promise, acquittal by a majority vote of the chapter, acquital for evil desires, and covering up the whole thing without going to details.

"Aananda, how are the proceedings done in the presence of the accused? The bhikkhu disputes, this is the Teaching and this is not the Teaching, this is the Discipline and this is not the Discipline. Then all the bhikkhus unite and get together and examine it according to the Teaching and should approve and settle it. Thus the proceedings are done in the presence of the accused."[1]

However, the social conflict that we often see happening rooted from a sense of social injustice and it usually promotes aggression or revenge. One can use violence as the only way to resolve social injustices they have suffered, and to ensure that their basic needs are met. This is especially ability if no forces continued support to strengthen the oppressive social structures or bring justice punishment or rehabilitation. But the system power has responded by trying to quell the disturbance and maintain the status quo. This could lead progression of violent conflict.

Conflicts use to focus on issues of justice tend intractable sick and most affected by self-interest. Nonetheless, each side often has its own justice in absolute terms, as some standards of independence and objectivity of justice to meet the needs of benefits. Linking with equal issues, many people have recognized the mutual dependence between closely violations of human rights and intractable conflicts. Violations of economic and political rights are a major cause

---

[1] Ibid...

of many serious crisis situations; thereby creating more abuse of human rights. When the human rights to adequate food, housing, employment and cultural life is denied, and the large group of human rights are excluded from the decision-making process of political and social institutions, and there potentially huge unrest to social society. Such conditions usually give rise to conflicts of justice, in which each side party requests their basic needs rights are met. Indeed, many conflicts arise and grow up due to violating human rights. For example, the massacre or torture could inflame hatred and consolidation of an enemy determined to continue fighting for his suffering and hatred; violations of fundamental rights also could lead to further violence from the other side, and can contribute to spiral pushing the conflicts still spreading out of control.

The different forms of economic events and oppression self-determination right usually lead to more the human tragedy in the circumstances of disease, hunger, and lack of shelter. In the case of serious violations of human rights, it is difficult to carry reconciliation talks from the conflict characters. This is not easy for every side to proceed to transformation the conflict and forgiveness together when memories of serious violence and crime are still in their thought.

In Sangha community, to prevent and resolve conflicts maybe occurred, the Buddha taught every monk must live in harmony, and practice the six principles of good karma with his body, speech and thought:

1. The action of the body should be directed to others with loving kindness
2. The action of the words must be directed to others with the loving kindness

3. Thought should be directed to others with the loving kindness

4. Equal sharing equality with food and belongings

5. Equality in moral disciplines

6. Sharing experiences to exterminate suffering and attain the real happiness

'Aananda, there are six things that promote unity, gladness and friendship, and dispel disputes. What are the six? Aananda, the Bhikkhu should be established in bodily actions of loving kindness towards co-associates in the holy life openly and secretly. The Bhikkhu should be established in verbal actions of loving kindness towards co-associates in the holy life openly and secretly. The Bhikkhu should be established in mental actions of loving kindness towards co-associates in the holy life openly and secretly. Again the Bhikkhu shares equally all rightful gains so far as the morsels put in the bowl, with the virtuous co-associates in the holy life. Again the Bhikkhu becomes equal in all virtues that are not spotted, fissured, free of blemish, and praised by the wise as conducive to concentration, with the co-associates in the holy life. Again the Bhikkhu shares the noble view that rightfully destroys unpleasantness, of one who logically thinks about it, with the co-associates in the holy life openly and secretly. Aananda, these six things promote unity, gladness and friendship and dispel disputes. Aananda, do you see a single word which is not acceptable among these words?

'Venerable sir, I do not see.'

'Therefore Aananda, be accomplished in these six things that promote unity, gladness and friendship and dispels disputes, it will be for your welfare for a long time."[1]

---

[1] Ibid...

4.2 VIOLENCE OF NEGATIVE EMOTIONS

In Dalai Lama book, 'The Art of Happiness' provides his analysis of the roots of violence. He points out that the roots of violence ultimately lead to our destructive emotions and their ability to distort our perception of reality. To understand the role of negative emotions and distortions in thinking as the main causes of violence better, it is useful to briefly consider what emotions, why we have them, and how they relate to the distortions of thinking. Firstly, although we believe that some of the emotions are negative, or destructive; it is important to remember that in the evolution of every human emotion has developed with a constructive purpose: from the point of view of evolution, all the emotions are designed to help us survive and leave offspring.

Emotions are emerged to prepare us to respond very quickly to the vital events. The word 'emotion' comes from the Latin word that expresses the idea of movement, and in general, all the emotions are an extremely effective mechanism to turn our attention to the situation and encourage us in the direction that is necessary for our well-being and survival. Destructive emotions in general were designed to help us to immediately respond to life-threatening situations - to react in a way so that our chances of survival increased. They tell us that something, which is 'bad', has already happened or is about to happen, and suggest a certain course of actions. In fact, they highly recommend a certain course of actions. Of course, there are emotions they play other useful roles, especially in communication where they help to inform others of our inner state through the characteristic facial expressions or gestures.[1]

Chagdud Rinpoche suggested that, to understand how the emotions incur, follow your thinking.

---

[1] Dalai Lama and Howard C. Cutler. 'The Art of Happiness'

At first let it simply relaxes - try not thinking in the past or future, not feel hope or fear about this thing or the other thing, so let it rest comfortably open and natural. In this open space of the mind, no problem, no suffering.

And then focus your attention - an image, a sound, a smell…, your thought splits into inner and outer, self and other, subject and object; such awareness is simply the object, and no problems.

But when your thought have nothing, you realize that it's large or small, black and white, square and circle, and then you distinguish it. For example, whether it is beautiful or ugly, after you start distinguishing about it, you immediately react to it: you decide you like it or not like it. That's when the problems started; because 'I like it' leads to 'I want it.' We want to possess what we feel that like it. Likewise, 'I don't like it' leads to 'I do not want it.' If we like something, want it, and cannot have it, then we suffer. If we don't like it, but don't let it go, so we suffer again. Our suffering seems to occur for the object of negative desires (pleasures), aversion (unpleasant) within us, but the essence of things is not like that - it happens because the mind is split into two sides of the object and the subject and becomes involved in 'like' or 'dislike' something.

We often think that the only way to create happiness is to try to control the external circumstances of our lives, and try to fix what seems wrong or to get rid of everything annoys and that hurt us. But the real problem lies in our reaction to those circumstances. What we have to change is our mind and how it experiences in problems of reality. (Gates to Buddhist Practice)

According basis of brain anatomy evolved in the Pleistocene era, a period when our environment was much more hostile to us than it is now. The main negative emotions - fear, disgust, anger, sadness - were developed as a very effective solution to combat persistent problems faced by our distant ancestors. Each of these emotions has its own adaptive function. For example, fear helps us to respond to the threat or danger; disgust, with its main motivation to push away - which was designed to help us avoid infection or reject a potentially poisonous food; anger, of course, helped to prepare to fight or attack, but could also serve as a warning signal when something prevents us; and sadness, probably encouraged us to take the necessary time out to regroup after a defeat, to be careful to protect our forces, and without a doubt, it has also appealed to other people's help. Thus, every emotion has its own purpose or objective, so that each is associated with feelings, thinking and behavior, and characteristic for it which is specially built to help us achieve certain goals.[1]

Since most of these negative emotions were designed to help us to cope with critical or life-threatening situations where the fraction of a second is ultimately important; they have to get us to move very quickly and decisively. In this kind of dangerous situations we do not have time to consciously analyze the problem in depth, so that the emotions get stuck even before the information is completely processed in the neocortex - the new cerebral cortex, the center of the thinking processes. Place of negative emotions is the limbic system, in places such as the amygdala, which is responsible for the call of emotions like fear or hostility. Discomfort is caused by negative emotions serve a good service, attracting our attention to what is happening, forcing us to make sure that we are attentive to what we do, and moving us in the direction of resolving the situation. The sense of impending

---

[1] Ibid...

catastrophe that is inherent to fear, for example, can be quite painful, but it is precisely this pain that ensures our full attention, encourages us not to linger on, and triggers us for preventive actions.

Of course, emotions are associated not only with the feeling; each emotion also causes changes in the way of thinking and characteristic changes in the body. Messages sent by neurons in the neocortex of the limbic system may affect our way of thinking. There are also complex connections between the limbic system and other parts of the brain, as well as the various organs in the body. Messages sent via neural pathways or networks that can cause rapid changes throughout the body. With regard to these physical changes, every negative emotion associated with a particular propensity to action is a sequence of physiological changes that mobilize support for specific actions which are intended to prepare us for the reaction to danger or to help us to ensure our salvation.

To understand this process better, we can take fear as an example. It is our defense mechanism that warns us of the danger in particular on life-threatening situations; and like other emotions, it prepares us to respond quickly to provide our salvation. So how does it do it? As soon as our senses perceive a potential threat, sensory information is sent to the amygdala, which primarily provides our motivation to action in creating an unpleasant feeling of impending disaster. Then it prepares our body to the point: immediately messages are sent to the neural network, in some cases reaching a direct effect on the target organs, and in other cases by stimulating glands to produce chemical messages - hormones that travel through the bloodstream to the other target organs.

These messages give rise to a cascade of effects throughout the body, and each of them prepares the body to do what is necessary for survival: heart rate and blood pressure rise to prepare for our action. Breathing quickens to deliver more oxygen; muscles tense; the perception intensifies; sweat begins to flow when the body needs a little evaporative cooling after a hard run; stress hormones such as adrenaline and cortisol to course through the body. These hormones increase the vital functions, directing the flow of blood to the muscles, and especially the large muscles of the legs and arms to preparing us to fight or flee. They mobilize our energy reserves, releasing glucose from the liver for a quick drive, and even cause changes in the blood platelets to provide rapid blood clotting in case of injury. At the same time, messages are sent that disable unimportant function, temporarily suspending the activity of the digestive system, the reproductive system, and immune system - after all, if you are persecuted by bloodthirsty maniac with an ax, then your brain realizes that maybe this is not the perfect time for an afternoon sex, delicious food digestion or for the performance of household chores on the farm, such as the production of antibodies to fight infection (Howard C. Cutler).

These physiological changes are often called a response or reaction to stress. They can help us to prepare for the usual protective action, or more specific types of behavioral responses in depending on the nature of the danger. Such reactions include running or aggression - if a person cannot escape fading or shackling of action is another potential reaction to the fear, which can be useful if a person is close to the fall from a cliff, or if the best means of salvation will be disguise, and in some cases it can even suppress the reflex to attacking some predators.

We can see how these physical changes associated with negative emotions; can be quite useful in situations for which they are intended - the situations that are dangerous to life.

However, in a certain sense, these changes can be seen as imposing limits or tapers that impact on our behavior. This tendency to action is programmed by physiological changes in the body associated with emotions, and pushing the person to a particular course of action, such as fighting, fleeing, vomiting (associated with emotion of disgust), and so on. We still can choose any action although the emotion of fear, for example, can prepare the body to escape, We do not have to run away, and we can even decide to sing an aria or lie down to sleep. But our course of action in this case is 'narrowed' in the sense that the body is put on alert for more limited and specific course of actions.

Of course, in addition to the physical effects, negative emotions can also affect our way of thinking. The combination of effects on the body and the mind sometimes is called thought-effective addiction. Negative emotions tend to distort our thinking, reaching a certain 'narrowing' effect on the perception, as well as they have a narrowing effect on our behavior. Thus, we can say that negative emotions have the same effect on the narrowing of our thought-effective addiction.[1]

On the narrowing of our thought-effective addiction, someone also cannot see anything true to its essence; they continue jumping under negative emotions such as happy, sad ... and still dissolute living to the desires arising from within never stop.

> "As creeping ivy craving grows
> In one living carelessly
> Like this, one leaps from life to life
> As ape in the forest seeking fruit."[2]

---

[1] Ibid...

[2] DhP334/Translated from Pali by Ven. Weragoda Sarada Maha Thero

(Manujassa pamattacarino
Tanha vaddhati maluva viya
So plavati hurahuraj
Phalam icchaj va vanasmi vanaro.)

The most important question is how negative emotions and their narrowed mindset that prompts a distorted and incorrect perception of reality in leading to violence and destructive behavior. To answer this question, it is useful to first take a closer look at the specific changes in thinking caused by destructive emotions.

Scientific researchers have provided quite ample evidence that negative emotions in general have a 'narrowing' effect on our thinking. This makes sense if we remember the reason why negative emotions emerged in the course of evolution. In situations that are dangerous to life, our chances to survive are above all, and we are able to send all of our cognitive capabilities to solve one problem at hand. We send all the attention, all the resources of the brain and the ability to think on how to survive in a particular situation at the short moment. So, in fact, in these situations, thinking and perception are narrowed: restricted with the actual problem, focused on the present moment.

Through vijñaptimātravāda (cittamā-travāda, yogācāra) - school of Consciousness in the field of Buddhist psychology, the cognitive narrow thinking can be called Manas Consciousness (末那識/ mano-Vijnana) or Root of all Consciousness. It is one of eight main consciousnesses in the human consciousness stream, also known as clinging ego - afflicted mentality. Its nature is psychological dependence, negative and including good and bad and neutral. The most important feature of this consciousness is attachment to Alaya consciousness (阿陀那識, ādāna-vijñāna) as is its See of part or life. Manas clings

Alaya's subject and object perceptions as same as itself, and it prevent Alaya's free actives in the transformation of good seeds. Manas also known as born together clinging ego (俱生我執 - sahaja -ahaṃkāra-manaskāratāa) - the ego follows Alaya consciousness to born once. According trimṣikā-vijñaptimātratā, Manas is self-conservative, self -delusion, self-pride, and self-craving. The Mana' activities are 'moving' (usually moving like waterfall stream) - its operation is very fast as flowing water; because its nature is self-craving also, so the Manas protects ego 'born together' of itself very sensitive in all situations unexpected even in moments of thinking.

Therefore, in dangerous situations, where even a fraction of a second counts, speed and decisiveness are critical in resolving it. To increase the chances of survival, the brain has no time to send the information up into the upper thinking centers of the neocortex, requiring time to analyze the situation, and a measured and deliberate decision of which a course of action is suitable best of all. Instead, we are automatically programmed to respond, relying on a more primitive brain mechanism. The brain wants to quickly categorize something with which you are faced, relying on simple paired category black or white, safe or risky, and so on. This way of thinking will save up your cognitive resources to ensure that you act quickly and effectively, and so on, but for this you will have to pay attention: you may focus your thinking on the threat right before your eyes to increase their chances of survival, but only at the expense of long-term thinking, that thinking for a long time in future. According to scientific analysis, the way of thinking to react quickly is the expense of being able to see the 'grey 'areas' (Cutler). But to Buddhist psychology, Manas gets measure to make its nature and shapes. Beacause its essence is constant thoughts considerations, calculations, measurements never interrupted; thefore, it can able to protect the ego (Self defence) is very clever and quick as a lightning.

However, this kind of fast thinking scores on reasoning, logic, and critical judgment, but largely bypassing the top centers in the brain thinkin gor the positive sides of Manas. This explains why changes in our way of thinking caused by negative emotions are limiting our ability to find solutions to our problems. This also explains why such a way of thinking and special ability prevents us come to an understanding or a compromise - when we try to successfully resolve our conflicts without the aid of violence that Dalai Lama enlightens the most.

Such 'narrative' ways of thinking, inherent in all negative emotions, but as already mentioned, each of the negative emotions has been specifically designed to help deal with the danger of a certain kind. The negative emotion is also a kind of distinguish of Manas in playing of role acts of self-defense instinct. Therefore, in addition to the general narrowing effect of the negative emotions, each of them has its own specific influence on thinking distortions, which effect on human judgment and decision-making that can serve as the hallmark of the other negative emotions. Manas clings to Alaya to create energy in making good and bad seeds of good and expressing on thingkings of consciousness. The habitual behavior as attachment, anger, jealousy... arise all, and they a source of our energy to order us acting, speech and thought in negatively. As each emotion is associated with a certain way of human judgment about what is happening around at all, and with a characteristic tendency to make certain choices or to take certain decisions, it could be seen as another kind of distortion or restriction of thinking.

For example, distortions of thinking caused by anger, well documented, and can serve as a good example of a more specific narrowing and distorting effects of negative emotions. Extensive studies have confirmed that when angry people think about a situation or a person, or when they seek to solve the problem; they tend to over simplify the facts to think very quickly and superficially, and to make conclusions too fast. In such way, their thinking is narrowed or restricted by the fact that they do not pay attention to the details and avoid deeper research and analysis. It easily can be distinguished, for example, from the distorting influence of sadness as sad people process information through concentration on detail, and they can engage in more in-depth analysis, but do not pay attention to the complete picture, and can selectively focus on the information that reinforces their sad mood. In making decisions, angry people also tend to rely on a subconscious (Alaya) feeling of infallibility of their evidence, or opinions that can lead to a sense of confidence and optimism, but at the same time may weaken their ability to be objective and reasonable.

A Buddha'story following about not-reacting to anger will help us better understanding to Buddha's great confidence of wisdom:

… Angry and displeased, [Bharadvaja the Abusive] approached the Buddha [Gotama] and abused and reviled him with rude, harsh words.

When he had finished speaking, the Buddha said to him: "What do you think, Brahmin (Bharadvaja)? Do your friends and colleagues, kinsmen and relatives, as well as guests come to visit you?"

"Sometimes they come to visit, Master Gotama"

"Do you then offer them some food or a meal or a snack?"

"Sometimes I do, Master Gotama."

"But if they do not accept it from you, then to whom does the food belong?"

"If they do not accept it from me, then the food still belongs to us."

"So too, Brahmin, we - who do not abuse anyone, who do not scold anyone, who do not rail against anyone - refuse to accept from you the abuse and scolding and tirade you let loose at us. It still belongs to you, Brahmin! It still belongs to you, Brahmin!

"Brahmin, one who abuses his own abuser, who scolds the one who scolds him, who rails against the one who rails at him - he is said to partake of the meal, to enter upon an exchange. But we do not partake of your meal; we do not enter upon an exchange. It still belongs to you, Brahmin! It still belongs to you, Brahmin!"

> ... One who repays an angry man with anger
> Thereby makes things worse for himself.
> Not repaying an angry man with anger,
> One wins a battle hard to win...

As is often the way in these stories, in the end Bharadvaja is transformed by his encounter with the Buddha, becomes a monk, and, under the Buddha's guidance, eventually achieves complete awakening.[1]

These tendencies can be traced back to the most basic functions of anger - when the ego is scorned, our plans are thwarted or something prevented us to reach the goal, and anger bursts to remove the obstacle. The reason is perceived as something external, with which we have to fight or what we have to overcome. Therefore, this general orientation as the destruction of any threats or obstacles associated with

---

[1] From SN VII.2, Bhikkhu Bodhi

a tendency to see the external circumstances as the cause of the problem, and with a characteristic tendency to blame others whenever anger erupts. In fact, studies show that anger itself can automatically use thinking that leads to prejudice.

A new Buddhist technique for dealing with anger by Master Thich Nhat Hanh to reduce the risks of conflicts from within and outside us in following 5 simple steps:

Step 1: Mindfulness with the emotions

We can say to our anger,

- "Breathing in, I know that anger is in me. Breathing out, I know that I am my anger."

Or:

- "Breathing in, I know that anger is in me. Breathing out I know that I must put all my energy in order to take care of my anger."

When we are angry...

- We are the anger
- Do not judge or repress the anger
- Focus on the self, not on the other
- As an older sister cares for a younger sister,
- As a gardener sees with insight and non-dual vision the potential beauty of compost,
- Gradually we can transform the anger completely into peace, love, and understanding

To cool down:

Step 2: Take a walk outside, meditating

- Breathing in, I know that anger is here.
- Breathing out, I know that the anger is me.

- Breathing in, I know that anger is unpleasant
- Breathing out, I know this feeling will pass.
- Breathing in, I am calm.
- Breathing out, I am strong enough to take care of this anger.

Step 3: From understanding to compassion

- When we are calm enough to look directly at the anger, we can begin to see its root causes: misunderstanding, clumsiness, injustice, resentment, or conditioning.
- Taking time, perhaps half an hour, to be mindful of the anger, transforms it.
- "Seeing and understanding are the elements of liberation that bring about love and compassion."

Step 4: Realizing about the roots of anger

The primary roots are in ourselves:

- Our lack of understanding of these causes of anger
- Our desire, pride, agitation, and suspicion

The secondary roots are in the other. When we understand the factors that led to the other's behavior, we can respond with help or discipline from a place of compassion.

Step 5: Becoming free of knots

- We learn to become aware of problematic reactions, handling them promptly and easily in the present.
- We learn to let past problematic experiences come to mindfulness.
- Practicing of breathing and smiling, we learn to look at our difficult emotions without having to turn away from them, seeing the associations based on past experience.[1]

---

[1] Thích Nhat Hanh's steps of mindfulness

When negative emotion and anger are not transformed, this also could be a reason for angry people to be more prone to punitive measures for any possibility to harm others. For example, in one study, the anger was caused to a group of people who after that were asked to evaluate a series of fictitious court cases that they have nothing to do with the problems that have angered them, and the people in anger were much more inclined to accuse the defendants and recommend tougher punishment. This experiment also indicated a very problematic aspect of destructive emotions: their impact on the thinking and behavior is quite stable, and it is seamlessly transferred to other situations that have nothing similar with the original event that gave rise to these emotions. There is a huge amount of scientific data proving that the subsequent judgment or decision of the person would be rather affected by negative emotions, than not, even if the person does not know about it. For example, research of office workers in their production environment that the object's irritation flows on his judgements about co-workers and acquaintances, so that angry participants in the study were less likely to trust them even though they had nothing cognate with the cause of those humans anger. In such cases, as long as the person does not get rid of the destructive emotions, it will have a tendency, or "cognitive predisposition" to see subsequent events through the unconscious lens of perception. And, as it known, when a person perceives events and information at all in a distorted form, this will certainly have some effect on its judgments and decisions.

Thus, according to Dalai Lama words, destructive emotions can cause changes in thinking, which seek to distort and obscure the reality. The Dalai Lama explained how some of these common distortions of thinking, such as the lack of awareness about the long-term consequences of our actions, thinking "black or white", the failure to look at the deeper issues related to the problem, and so on, are able to become the sources of the biggest part of human misery and suffering. In talking about the relationship between the destructive emotions and distorted thinking, he also raised another important question, not only destructive emotions rise to distortions of thinking, but also to distortions of thinking can cause destructive emotions, so as we see, it works in both directions. This is very important, because if such factors like influence of social environment, strong propaganda, different leaders trying to manipulate, or the terms of the situation at all are distorting act on someone's way of thinking and perception under certain conditions it can cause or contribute to destructive emotions - such as anger and hatred - with potentially catastrophic consequences.[1]

4.3 CONFLICTS OVER NATURAL RESOURCE

The world today is on the fragile edge between keeping peace and starting war. It all started with the industrial and technological revolution. The modern age is marked by unwarranted optimism about the development of science and technology. It is believed that they lead us to a brighter future. This is the main feature of modernity that reflects the contemporary approach - reliance on knowledge, technology and science; in general, that gives rise to a feeling of confidence in the future which implies such a thing as progress. And under progress it means the ability to produce different things of higher quality and wider scale. For that promise there use of natural resources is at maximum, and these resources are then processed by industry with a help of

---

[1] Dalai Lama and Howard C. Cutler. 'The Art of Happiness'

advanced technologies. The result is a society based on mass production and consumption.

By studying modern history, we see that scientific industrial progress is always accompanied by constant wars. An integral component of this progress is the colonization, the struggle for natural resources and the monopoly; those countries that achieve the greatest success in this fight are considered rich, developed and advanced. They are called leading superpowers. But the reality is that the basic idea of modernity cannot stand the test of time and cause serious doubts. Alternative views are increasingly distributed and shared by majority of thinking people.

There are several major problems that humanity faces which are the most obvious manifestations of the global crisis. This contributes to the buildup of weapons and to the great attention to research in the field of military technology which is the main task of advanced science. In addition, the idea that by controlling the space you can control the world is still not outdated. Despite the fact that the conquest of space requires a lot of financial, technical and scientific resources, it is actively continuing.

Numerous armed conflicts start because of the clash of geopolitical interests in the struggle for natural resources. This is the reality of what is happening today in the Middle East, Iraq, and in Afghanistan. Central Asia is quite deeply mired in the new post-Soviet geopolitical games in the struggle for spheres of influence. Natural resources are the main source of energy today; those are still oil and gas. But we all know that oil reserves are very limited. Therefore, among the major multinational companies, and also among the largest monopolies in the world, now started the final battle for survival in it will be determined who in the next twenty, thirty or fifty will get the remaining deposits of natural resources. The war in Iraq began in fact because of it. And many so-called conflicts between civilizations, of which the biggest conflict - the conflict between the West and the Islamic world (it became a symbol of the terrorist attacks of 11 September 2001 in New York and Washington) is deepened. For years, there is a war against terrorism in Afghanistan and Iraq headed by America. But the situation is getting worse, and in the foreseeable future it seems to have no way out. Hatred and violence is spreading, and even politicians do not undertake to predict exactly what will be the end of this conflict.

The problem of violence is perhaps the most urgent, painful problem of our time. Every day people die and violence increases by spiral. And the main reason of it is rooted in the old hidebound way of thinking, characteristic of the modern era, and coupled with faith in materialism and technological development. There is an endless consumption of natural resources, recycling, mass production, sale in the market, consumption, refining, capital accumulation, and increasing of the 'well-being' and the 'standard of living'. This way of thinking is actually already outlived itself, but people do not think to change it. Therefore, violent conflicts are the most obvious, the primary problem, the cause of which lies in a false thinking and false values.

And how to get rid of the cause of which lies in a false thinking? Buddha said that looking at it and transforming it:

"And as I remained thus heedful, ardent, & resolute, thinking imbued with sensuality arose in me, I discerned that 'Thinking imbued with sensuality has arisen in me, and that leads to my own affliction or to the affliction of others or to the affliction of both. It obstructs discernment, promotes vexation, & does not lead to Unbinding.

"As I noticed that it leads to my own affliction, it subsided. As I noticed that it leads to the affliction of others... to the affliction of both... it obstructs discernment, promotes vexation, & does not lead to Unbinding, it subsided. Whenever thinking imbued with sensuality had arisen, I simply abandoned it, dispelled it, and wiped it out of existence.

"And as I remained thus heedful, ardent, & resolute, thinking imbued with harmfulness arose in me. I discerned that 'Thinking imbued with harmfulness has arisen in me; and that leads to my own affliction or to the affliction of others or to the affliction of both. It obstructs discernment, promotes vexation, & does not lead to Unbinding.'

"As I noticed that it leads to my own affliction, it subsided. As I noticed that it leads to the affliction of others... to the affliction of both... it obstructs discernment, promotes vexation, & does not lead to Unbinding, it subsided. Whenever thinking imbued with harmfulness had arisen, I simply abandoned it, dispelled it, and wiped it out of existence.

"When the mind was thus concentrated, purified, bright, unblemished, rid of defilement, pliant, malleable, steady, & attained to imperturbability, I directed it to the knowledge of the ending of the mental fermentations. I discerned, as it had come to be, that 'This is stress... This is the origination of stress... This is the cessation of stress... This is the way leading to the cessation of stress... These are fermentations... This is the origination of fermentations... This is the cessation of fermentations... This is the way leading to the cessation of fermentations.' My heart, thus knowing, thus seeing, was released from the fermentation of sensuality, released from the fermentation of becoming, released from the fermentation of ignorance. With release, there was the knowledge, 'Released.'"[1]

---

[1] Dvedhavitakka Sutta: translated from the Pali by Thanissaro Bhikkhu

4.4 THE RELATIONSHIP BETWEEN LIVING BEINGS AND ENVIRONMENT

Apart form that, also, can we exploit nature and natural resources to infinity from our ignorance? We cannot because the nature itself is telling us that it is impossible. They are limited, and in addition, planet Earth is a public property of all creatures living on it. No one can argue that natural resources belong to them personally. Nature and its riches is not someone's property. Therefore, a new look and a new way of thinking in ecology can be expressed in the following short sentence: 'we hold the planet and natural resources in obligation to the future generations, and this cannot be our property'. The natural resources of the planet we must preserve and protect as a treasure to our children and grandchildren. This is a completely new idea, contrary to the modern conventional thinking. The real causes of all wars are rooted in a false idea that derived from the colonial era, imperialism and socialism: the idea that you can endlessly use natural resources, because nature is boundless. But the planet says that it cannot give it any longer. And if the planet dies, then along with it, of course, all life will end. For the first time in many years, modern science has come to a new, wiser vision that is not how to exploit nature and to win it, but to establish the relationship between nature and our existence.

In the past two millennia, humanity has not experienced a truly serious threat to their survival. As we begin this millennium, there is an increasingly worsening crisis in the earth's environment, and this has aroused a real threat to human existence on a global scale. It is likely that the earth's ecosystem will degenerate if environmental degradation will not be reversed.

Degeneration of the earth will leave the earth's ecosystem in a state of imbalance which will render it impossible for the human race to exist. Environmental problems continue to expand in scale through environmental problems like marine pollution, green house gasses and the destruction of forests to a large extent due to the materialistic civilization which has been fuelled by advances in science and technology. Humanity has to therefore re-examine their lifestyles and ethical values regarding living with nature if it is ever to break free the hold of this destructive cycle.[1]

As the issue of environmental pollution continues to pose a threat to our health through global warming and climate change, it has led to increased awareness of environmental protection globally. However, this is among the basic laws that were set out by Buddha about 25 centuries ago for Buddhists to follow. For the thousands of years that Buddhism has existed, the Buddhist forest monasteries being established in the forests and mountains have manifested harmonious living with nature. [2]

Due to the notion that Buddhism represents a way of compassion, the founder of the Buddhist faith entrenched a total compassion, and thus he is therefore respectfully viewed as the protector of all beings, who is also compassionate. Buddha's teachings to his followers stressed on the practice of loving-kindness to avoid harming any form of life on earth. According to this doctrine, protecting all forms of life is not only good for the wellbeing of mankind, but also for the protection of animals and vegetation. This Buddhist philosophy therefore views all life forms in the universe as equal entities in nature, and in this world, the lives of all

---

[1] Damien, K., The Nature of Buddhist Ethics (2003)

[2] Barua, M., & Basilio, Buddhist Approach to Protect the Environment in Perspective of Green Buddhisst

people, animals and plants is interrelated, dependent on each other, and has to develop in a mutual fashion.[1]

In order to study how Buddhism and environmental protection are interrelated, it is essential to first consider the concept of inevitability in Buddhist doctrines. In Buddhist philosophy, environmental problems are not inevitable, expletive or essential Early Buddhist philosophies consider the environment that we live in or the natural phenomena that we experience as suffering, void, impermanence and non-self, and the incomprehensible form of nature's transitory state.[2]

Currently, Buddhism recognizes nature as fundamental to life through a positive manner. For example, Buddhist concepts like the non-duality of life and its environment and the origination in dependence are commonly referred to in Buddhist teachings. This concept purports that life and its environment are in essence two very different phenomena, but also that they are non-dual in the basic sense. The other fundamental Buddhist ideology is known as the origination in dependence concept which poses that any living entity does not exist and act independently, but rather every entity exists because of the relationship it has with others in the environment, or the conditions that relate to other entities within the earth. Essentially, these concepts from Buddhism bring out the precious value of the environment, as well as in the Buddhist view enables one to examine the environment and nature in general as an essential component of a complex and intricate balanced system. In addition, because environmental destruction is interconnected to personal destruction through the non-duality of life and

[1] Sahni, P., Environmental Ethics in Buddhism: A Virtues Approach

[2] Yamamoto, S., & Kuwahara, V., Symbiosis with the Global Environment: Buddhist Perspective of Environmental Education

its environment, preventing environmental degradation becomes fundamental.[1]

The consciousness-only doctrine in Mahayana Buddhism indicates that the eight Alaya-consciousness (alayashiki) in the realm of human's consciousness is interrelated to the physical world such as rivers, mountains forests and earth. Consequently, environmental destruction will definitely affect the deep human consciousness. Buddhism therefore points to an intricate relationship beyond a consciousness of human existence and their natural surroundings. Therefore, according to the Buddhist faith, environmental challenges will cause suffering while the environmental pollution and degradation undertaken by any being directly and indirectly affect the existence of all beings or form of life in the world. Because all life is affected, it is important to remove the affliction of environmental destruction in order for the theoretical way of practicing Bodhisattva to be attained.[2]

Currently, the desire of material things by humans can be said to be a necessary condition in order to maintain and develop the socioeconomic system in society. Therefore, environmental challenges are not only a depiction of evil or negative desires and passions, but they are viewed as a cause and manifestation of increasing negative passions. It is therefore necessary for the theoretical practice of Buddhism to overcome these negative passions, and to alter the socioeconomic system. The current Buddhist philosophy or ideology is that the occurrence of natural phenomena and environmental problems are inevitable. However, the purpose of Buddhism is to overcome these challenges as described above.[3]

---

[1] Ibid…

[2] Sahni, P., Environmental Ethics in Buddhism

[3] Barua, M., & Basilio, Buddhist Approach to Protect the Environment ….

How Buddhism Overcomes Environmental Challenges?

The social change that would enable humanity manage environmental challenges, or deal with natural phenomena that Buddhism offers proposes that it cannot be a radical revolution, but rather it should be a gradually sustained systematic change. The change that Buddhism offers is similar to a famous quote by a popular Buddhist monk in India known as Mahatma Gandhi; he stated that "Good travels at a snail's pace". It suggests that the accomplishment of a social revolution with regard to environmental challenges starts with one person. For every person to begin accepting environmental problems as their personal concern and education is vital. The Buddhist perspective suggests that education is the only tool/resource which can provide the impetus for this awareness when environmental problems begin to directly affect our lives as personal problems.[1]

It is therefore important for people to gain a deeper understanding and awareness of environmental challenges. From a Buddhist perspective, recognizing the occurrence of natural phenomena is justified by the doctrine of origination in dependence where everything in this world is connected. Thus the main principles for sustaining our world are essentially linked to symbiosis and biodiversity in nature. The Buddhist perspective further has the view that when we shall get to understand and be aware of nature and the causes of environmental problems we shall start to re-evaluate our present lifestyles while nurturing the foundations of values and ethics, thus enabling us to become responsible towards nature, as well as for other future generations. Finally, a substantial point for mitigating environmental challenges and incorporating Buddhism in such education is by ensuring that each individual takes personal responsibility with the

---

[1] Swearer, D., An Assessment of Buddhist Eco-Philosophy

aim of understanding the problem and being part of the solution.[1]

According to the Buddha's teaching, all kinds of types and forms of life, not only people, but of countless living beings manifested in different forms and depending on previous actions and karma. The way we act determines the conditions of our life. Our form and way of life, living conditions are the consequence of our actions and deeds. But our actions, in their turn, come from our consciousness. The way we think and perceive the world leads us to certain acts, and defining our lives and the ways in which it manifests itself. Everything is interconnected. Our thinking, actions and living conditions are linked. We are the result of our actions in terms of the physical and environmental conditions of our existence. There are conditions of our physical body and ecological environmental conditions that support our physical existence. Both of it is due to our actions, and the latter are defined by our state of consciousness. Our views and thoughts are the seeds from which all of our actions grow. And our actions determine the form of life and environmental conditions that accompany it.

> "No God, no Brahma can be found
> No matter of this wheel of life
> Just bare phenomena roll
> Depend on conditions all." (Visuddhi Magga)

All of this concerns not only the life in present, but is also related to the infinite past and passes on into the infinite future. This chain of depend on conditions in cause and effect circle has no beginning or end. From the point of view of science, it is believed that the universe was created as a result of the big bang or in some other way - there are many

---

[1] Damien, K., The Nature of Buddhist Ethics (2003)

different theories. At some stage of the process of development of the universe and our planet came with its various forms of life, from bacteria to mammals, and all these forms of life are the result of the evolution of the planet. But the planet itself is a part of the solar system and galaxy, where everything is closely interconnected. Without the universal evolution, there would not have been the planet Earth. And if it were not for the planet Earth, then there would be no system of life as we know it today.

As soon as this thin and delicate balance is destroyed, all living organisms will disappear, because none of them can exist independently. When the balance of power between the Earth and the Moon would be destroyed, it will lead to a planetary catastrophe. If in the solar system, for whatever reason, broken the path of movement, the Earth will be disturbed, for example, because of its entry into the comet with a large force of gravity, of course, it will be a planetary disaster, and life on the planet will disappear. By this we need to know how thin the existing natural cosmic balance and harmony is in the universe. No existence in it is independent and separate; everything is interconnected even on the smallest level. If we look at our body and internal organs of the system, we will see the whole; there are many parts that do not exist separately, and depend on each other. Whole and part are not separated, everything is interconnected and interdependent, and there is a wonderful balance. The body itself is space. Similarly, the Earth, the Sun and the Moon, the rhythms of lunar gravity, life and death, change of seasons, the movement of the wind, motion balance of warm and cold air, oceans, rivers and mountains - everything is interconnected, as a whole, is the so-called ecosystem, or more precisely is the biosphere. Without it, life would be impossible on the planet.

However, the planet we see being not merely the material according to the Buddhist perspective. On the article of Huffingtonpost in Apr 2012, the Dalai Lama has answered that:

"Even with all these profound scientific theories of the origin of the universe, I am left with serious questions: What existed before the big bang? Where did the big bang come from? What caused it? Why has our planet evolved to support life? What is the relationship between the cosmos and the beings that have evolved within it? Scientists may dismiss these questions as nonsensical, or they may acknowledge their importance but deny that they belong to the domain of scientific inquiry. However, both these approaches will have the consequence of acknowledging definite limits to our scientific knowledge of the origin of our cosmos. I am not subject to the professional or ideological constraints of a radically materialistic worldview."[1]

In Buddhism, our consciousness and actions lead not only to the appearance of a certain body shape, but also go the shape of the earth and the environment. The symbol of this process is as same as the lotus which has flowers, fruits and seeds that exist at the same time in unity, inseparable. Therefore, the lotus is a symbol of the relationship of the law of cause and effect: the roots, flowers and fruits.

The developing life form and the sphere which supports the existence of it are single. If our actions result in the killing and destruction of life, as they say, we go to hell. If we start a war, as a result, human dwellings will be destroyed, nature will be destroyed, and we will see only blood and fire, and the destruction of all life - such are the consequences of the war, leading not only to the physical destruction, but also to a change in the surrounding world.

---

[1] The Dalai Lama, Buddhism, Cosmology and Evolution

As Nichiren wrote, "If the minds of the people are impure, their land is also impure, but if their minds are pure, so is their land. There are not two lands, pure and impure in themselves. The difference lies solely in the good or evil of our minds."

Therefore, to the manifestation of the infinite greed, the pursuit of wealth and accumulation, the consequences in this case will be the disappearance of natural resources by the destruction of nature. If the forests disappear, rivers and seas are polluted, in such circumstances there cannot exist any form of life. And only when the pollution industry wastes bring considerable harm, we begin to understand that we cannot simply exploit nature to meet the blind greed. Nature will necessarily respond to our alienation. Fish will not be able to live in the rivers and seas, and birds will not be able to live in the air. Many life forms that have evolved over the endless cosmic evolution, such as occupying precious natural spaces disappear: for example, in the Amazon forests, which are being burnt because of modern production, unique species of plants and animals that do not live in any other places are doomed to disappear because of people. Herbs that could cure diseases that are considered incurable and that people may face in the near future are also dying. These extinct forms of life could give us any answer to help people in the better future.

The Differing Karmic Outcomes Sutra says:

"If sentient beings continually engage in the ten unwholesome actions, the impact felt will be that the environment will suffer. What are the ten unwholesome actions? First, the taking of lives causes the soil to be saturated with salt, and plants cannot grow. Second, stealing brings about harsh, cold weather and the proliferation of insects, causing crop failure and famine. Third, sexual misconduct causes storms, suffering, and natural disasters. Fourth, lying contaminates the physical environment, causing it to be filthy and smelly..."

Fo Guang Shan's worldwide lay service organization, Buddha's Light International Association (BLIA) has developed the connection between the spiritual environment inside and the natural environment outside experienced for many years. The two organizations put environment on an elevated position in the global peace issues. At the annual BLIA General Conference held on BLIA March 1992, a workshop to promote the protection of 'environment and spirituality' are discussed. Everyone is encouraged to start to be with 'beautifying ones' own mind and heart with those around them and then to center overlooking external into beautifying the environment.

The Twelve Ways instructions to practice making the inside and outside environment more beautiful as follows:

1. *Speak softly, avoid disturbing others.*
2. *Keep the ground clean, eliminate littering.*
3. *Keep the air clean, do not smoke or pollute.*
4. *Respect self and others, avoid committing violent acts.*
5. *Be polite, avoid intruding upon others.*
6. *Smile; avoid facing others with an angry expression.*
7. *Speak kindly, avoid uttering abusive words.*
8. *Follow the rules; do not seek exemptions or privileges.*
9. *Mind your actions; avoid violating the rules of ethics.*
10. *Consume consciously, do not waste.*

11. Live with a purpose, avoid living aimlessly.

12. Practice kindness, avoid creating malicious thoughts.

Another way to conserve natural resources is to recycle old appliances. We may recycle paper, aluminum cans, plastic bottles and glass jars. By practicing recycling, we also practice the teachings of Buddha, strengthen the connection between people, and help people to improve awareness and action for our environment.

Here are some specific actions that we can perform:

- Consume moderately and do not buy more than you need. Excess food often rots and has to be thrown away.

- Maintain your car and follow emission guidelines.

- Minimize the use of disposable plates and utensils.

- Use glasses or mugs instead of paper cups.

- Take briefer showers.

- Do not litter and reduce the amount of trash.

- Use energy-efficient light bulbs and appliances.

- Set the air conditioner to a higher temperature.

- Recycle used newspapers and motor oil.

- Bring your own shopping bags when shopping.

- Inspect your car tires regularly. Tires with low pressure wear more quickly and lower fuel efficiency.

- Choose durable and fuel efficient tires.

- Use your car's air conditioner as little as possible. Automobile air conditioning systems are one of the main emitters of chlorofluorocarbons into the earth's ozone layer.

- Choose recycled materials, when possible.[1]

---

[1] Protecting Our Environment - Master Hsing Yun

Buddhism has always emphasized the interconnection, interdependence. Our minds and our actions are determined not only by the shape of our lives, but along with it by the natural environment, the biosphere, by which life is maintained and developed. The baby before birth is growing and developing in the womb, but this process continues also after birth, when the nature itself replaces mother's womb.

4.5 POTENTIAL WAR FROM MODERN WEAPONS

Although peace in the whole world is impossible without the prohibition of nuclear weapons, the prohibition is in no way synonymous with peace throughout the world in the truest sense of the word. Nuclear weapons are not the only weapon in the arsenals of sovereign states. There are many other weapons, some of them are hardly less terrible than nuclear, and even if a nuclear war would be impossible; nevertheless, it could cause irreparable damage to civilization and generate unprecedented suffering of humanity. If we want to achieve peace in the full sense of the word, we need to work in order to destroy not only nuclear weapons, but also conventional weapons. We do not want to eliminate nuclear weapons only to be in a situation like today, but without nuclear weapons. We also do not want to destroy it but to return to the situation of yesterday or the day before yesterday. Although, of course, it would be unsaid relief for humanity, the elimination of nuclear weapons by no means is enough. It is not enough even in the case of destruction of the two types of weapons both nuclear and non-nuclear. Peace in the full sense of the word can be achieved only if the disputes among sovereign states, as well as between smaller groups and individuals, will be settled exclusively by non-violent means.

The Buddha used to say about the three origins of evil or the 'three poisons' of greed, hatred, and ignorance which lead people going a dark road, so cannot realize what the true value of life is.

If what we do is driven by the poisons, the inevitable result is suffering. The suffering is not only at the individual level, but it involves another persons; it reflects its image in the actions of the community and society.

So when politics and economics based on negative thoughts and worst of human, the inevitable result is the society being rife with inequality and violence.

Buddhist's concern is also an incentive to promote sheds new light on the key questions of our time: the destruction of the environment, human exploitation, and the use of deception to quell the dissent and debate by human selfishness.

To achieve a peace in the whole world in a full sense of this word, we have to deepen our understanding of indivisibility of mankind and act for the sake of this understanding with even more consistency. We have to see ourselves as citizens of the world in a more specific sense than earlier and get rid of any taint of nationalism. We have to indentify ourselves more closely with all living beings and love everything that lives with a higher degree of unselfishness. Our voice of common sense and compassion for the world has be louder and clearer than ever before. We have to also apply to governments and peoples of the world, as well as to ourselves; the same pressure that is required for the prohibition of nuclear weapons, but even more persistent. And above all, we need to cultivate our devotion to the great moral and spiritual principle of non-violence, which applies both to relations between individuals, and relations between groups.

Already at the dawn of history or maybe it started with

the current cosmic cycle, in the world there were two great principles: the principle of violence and the principle of non-violence or as we might call the latter, the principle of love; however, in the sense of the Greek evangelical 'agape', not eros. The principle of violence is expressed in the use of force and deception, and such things as the oppression, exploitation, intimidation, and blackmail. Principle of non-violence or no harm (ahimsa) is reflected in friendliness, openness, and such qualities as courtesy, compassion, encouragement, empathy, and willingness to help. The principle of violence implies a reaction in response; ultimately it is destructive; the principle of non-violence means a creative attitude. The principle of violence is a principle of darkness; the principle of non-violence is a principle of light.

To live according to the principle of violence is to be either a beast, or the devil, or a cross between the two while to live according to the principle of non-violence is to be a human in the full sense of the word, or even an angel. Of course, people still live more according to the principle of violence than non-violence. It happened because it was possible to follow the principle of violence and not destroy yourself completely; however, it is not so anymore. Due to the appearance of superpower possessing nuclear weapons on the world stage, now it has become impossible to live according to the principle of violence, because in this case, sooner or later we will destroy ourselves.

Because of that, we are faced with the need to either learn to live in accordance to the principle of of non-violence, or cease to live at all. So, the real possibility of a nuclear disaster not only allows us to understand the true nature of the violence, what might be the consequences of violence that overgrown to the maximum, but also gives us a much deeper understanding of the true value of non-violence.

"We the unhating live
Happily midst the haters
Among the hating humans
From hatred dwell we free."[1]

(Susukhaj vata jivama
Verinesu averino
Verinesu manussesu
Viharama averino).

"By harming living beings
One is not a 'Noble' man,
By lack of harm to all that live
One is called a 'Noble One'."[2]

(Na tena ariyo hoti
Yena panani hijsati
Ahijsa sabbapananaj
Ariyo ti pavuccati.)

---

[1] DhP197/Translated from Pali by Ven. Weragoda Sarada Maha Thero

[2] DhP270/Translated from Pali by Ven. Weragoda Sarada Maha Thero

5. THE BUDDHA'S FIVE MORAL PRECEPTS AS RULES OF PREVENTION FOR A NEW SOCIETY

*"Morality is of highest importance,
but for us, not for God."*

- Albert Einstein

In Buddhism, there are many ethical principles, but the basis of Buddhist morality is The Five Precepts. The Buddha's Five Precepts are set for every lay person to know what is right and is wrong. Five Precepts is also an important morality that make lay Buddhists shape the special personality for themselves, causing trust to others, and making peace and compassion to the family, community, society and all living beings.

The Five Precepts:

1. Panatipata veramani sikkhapadam samadiyami

I undertake the precept to refrain from destroying living creatures.

2. Adinnadana veramani sikkhapadam samadiyami

I undertake the precept to refrain from taking that which is not given.

3. Kamesu micchacara veramani sikkhapadam samadiyami

I undertake the precept to refrain from sexual misconduct.

4. Musavada veramani sikkhapadam samadiyami

I undertake the precept to refrain from incorrect speech.

5. Suramerayamajja pamadatthana veramani sikkhapadam samadiyami

I undertake the precept to refrain from intoxicating drinks and drugs which lead to carelessness.

The most famous scheme of the ethical behavior in Buddhism is 'five percepts'. Since Buddhism is divided into many sects, and not a whole religion as is common in the Western world, so many things in it are also different. For example, this "precepts" the Buddha gave to people, the five precepts, which are often found in the extended version of the eight or the ten precepts. So what is the difference between them and which one of them shall we trust? According to 'Abhisanda Sutta', the Buddha gave the five precepts to the beginners. The five precepts are the basic ones, from which should start everyone. This precept is not just a set of rules, though, when you read about them in literature related to Buddhism, you could think about such explanation: Too often, people depict the Buddha telling what people should not to do, and therefore it gives the impression that Buddhism is the same unpractical thing in modern society as the other religions. However, in reality, precepts are just a moral behavior patterns. They are a natural expression of some skillful mental states. Since this is so, we are able to determine to what level we have developed in these same conditions, simply checking our own behavior with the precepts.

For example, in western ethic there are elements, which are dating to the classic Greco-Romanian tradition and elements from Judeo-Christian tradition that is prevalent, of course. In this Christian ethics morality is traditionally understood as a kind of law. Moral obligations and rules is something placed by God. This is clearly illustrated in the Biblical story of the origin of the Ten Commandments. Moses went up on Mount Sinai, and there amid thunder and lightning received the Ten Commandments from God. This illustrating the idea of ethics like something was forced upon man, maybe even against his will by some external force or authority. Nowadays, most people of the western countries are not Christians in any reasonable sense. Nevertheless, they continue to represent the ethics and morality in the same spirit that is, as imposed on them from outside obligation, a commandment, which they are, and obliged to obey. Perhaps, we can describe the position of traditional morality as she instructs not to do what you want, and to do what you do not want, for reasons that are unknown for us.

On the other hand, we have eastern tradition which is quite different. According to the teachings of the Buddha, and according to all Buddhist traditions or sects, actions are right or wrong, or perfect or imperfect depending on the state of consciousness in which they were committed. In other words, the moral criterion here is not theological, and psychological. It is true that in the West we do not entirely alien to that idea even within Christianity. However, if we talk about Buddhist ethics, this is the only criterion. This criterion has universal applicability and strictly applied in a consistent manner in Buddhist communities.

In this regard, people studying Buddhism may ask: how can these images of modern society fit 'five precepts'? Do not they represent a set of moral rules laid down by the Buddha himself, which we should follow? The answer is this really 'set of instructions' that was explained and recommended by the Buddha, but it is not imposed on the authority by force, as the ten commandments of God. To understand this system, we need to understand firstly, that this is not a set of rules, and imposed on us by the Buddha. It is rather the criteria that we should apply ourselves to; because according to the Buddha's point of view, we cannot be perfect humanity if we act in contradiction to these five precepts. To be a human, that is not enough just to be born; to be a human is already a criterion. Five moral precepts is some kind of guide which accomplishment is the way to become human.

Let us illustrate this with the next example to the rejection of theft. In such case we could divide people who do not practice theft into three groups - three levels of ethical practice. Practice of this principle for most people based on the fear of the law. In every country without exception, there is a law which forbids stealing, so stealing is a crime punishable by the applicable law in every country. Many people do not steal because of the fear of the law. However, if they know that the act of theft will never be disclosed, the temptation to steal seems to be very strong.

If we talk about the second level of ethical practice, there is a person should follow some religious teachings. In every great religion in the world believers are asked not to steal (to abstain from stealing). This second category of persons, of course, one is better than the first one. Because of their faith, they would not steal even if he steal act will never be disclosed. In fact, when we talk about the five principles, in order to be a real human, we must strive to third level of practice, namely, to seek to the complete freedom from the whole desire of stealing something.

When talking about the third level of ethical practice exercises, we want to mention the person who doesn't desire to steal whatever though in any whatsoever conditions. That is what we mean about reaching a standard that was established by the Buddha in these five principles. The same applies to the remaining four precepts. We have to understand firstly that the rejection of stealing is not a goal; this is means of achieving of human being. Oftenly, someone claim that, before they met Buddhism teachings, they felt that they were free to do almost everything; subsequently, they became feeling some kind of bounded with five precepts inter alia. They think that the purpose of the study and practice of Buddhism is to destroy suffering and achieve happiness, but what they feel is happening to them is seems to be something opposite. After they came into the contact with Buddhism, they began to feel that because of 'restrictions'. The reason for such feelings being they frequently take the means for the goal as the goal. When we follow the moral principles by our own free will, we understand that one day our behavior naturally comes to terms with the five moral principles (we will be able to behave naturally in accordance with the five precepts). Let us use as the example of learning of any foreign language in such way it would be easier to understand what I meant. To learn the language, first of all, we have to invest a lot of effort into the study of grammar. However, the study of grammar is not the ultimate goal. The ultimate goal is the ability to speak well and to write in this language as well as. When you are well trained in grammar, you will not violate the rules of grammar when you speak or write. You will have no grammatical mistakes.

So, the one who is enlightened, who reached the Buddhahood, who implanted the fullness of wisdom on himself, and who was filled with compassion will do all the things in some certain way, because that is the nature of enlightenment - to do so. Moreover, the more you are enlightened, more you want to do so, according to the Buddha's teachings. In case if you are not enlightened, or enlightened not that much, compliance of five precepts will help you to get through - the way that enlightened people are usually expressed in the personal experience of the state of mind. We will say this: the enlightened one who becomes a Buddha is free from the passionate desire or selfish desire, and at the same time most of us are full of such things; however, it would be harder for us to understand. For example, we entail for some sort of food, and we have some kind of special attachment to one or another kind of food. Suppose for the sake of the experiment, we stopped eating our favorite foods. Desire will gradually decrease, and at the end we will find that happy state in which there will be no craving for it, and then we will forget even to think about such things. Our failures no longer seem to be disciplinary punishment, but successfully becomes a true expression of the lack of desire as what we were sought to at the beginning.

Typically, five percepts are formulated negatively, so they just forbid some. However, for every instruction, there are also positive matches. Characteristic is that in the modern Buddhist teachings being negative instructions are much more popular than the positive ones. Many people have heard about five percepts, but hardly faced positive matches. In such context five positive matches could be called "five ethical principles."

Let us briefly examine the five precepts and their positive matching one after another - first the negative formulations and then positive ones. This will give us an adequate picture of the specific scheme of the Buddhist ethics.

5.1 THE PRECEPT TO REFRAIN FROM DESTROYING LIVING CREATURES

The first one of the five percepts is about 'abandoning the taking of life, abstains from taking life'. Although sometimes it is translating as 'thou shall not kill', but there is meant not only the refusal of the murder, but also the refusal of any other harm. It means giving up all forms of violence, oppression and corruption. Violence is unacceptable because it is ultimately based directly or indirectly on the unspent mental state, such as hatred and disgust. If we indulge to such of our unspent states, which are the natural expressions of violence, then these states will become even stronger and more powerful than before. [1]

Positive matching to harmlessness is the practice of 'Maitri' (Pali - metta) which means pure love and friendliness. Here 'maitri' is not just emotion or feeling; it is love which embodied in the practiced affairs. Feeling goodwill towards the others is not enough, 'maitri' must be expressed in actions. Otherwise, if we just enjoy the way we love others and what expression in our mind, which will not be pure enough. Therefore, we have to look after ourselves in this regard. Often we think that we already love other people or at least some of them; but if we test ourselves, we will find that we never show our love: it seems self-evident that all this has already been understood. People are not required to consider our feelings towards them for granted itself, or to imagine that we have some feelings or some relation to them. It should be fully manifested in our words and deeds. We absolutely must make concrete steps in order to maintain the spirit of love and friendship. That is why in the life of society and in Buddhist social life especially highly valued activities such as exchange of gifts or visits. It is not enough to sit in your own room, or even in your own cell to emit thoughts that are full of love. Perhaps, this also would be good, even great, but everything must find its concrete expression. Only then other people will respond to you aloud in a similar manner.

Positive acts in the practice of 'Maitri' by concrete actions that are capable of building peace in the truest sense. Maintaining Buddhist moral rules as same as maintaining

---

[1] Bhikkhu, AN 8.39

a principle of life that come from traditional and ancient human. Practicing the first precept, in addition to not killing living beings, we have to respect and protect for all beings' life, so that we also reap our actions back to our own happiness; that is also the most valuable gift in this world:

"There is the case where a disciple of the noble ones, abandoning the taking of life, abstains from taking life. In doing so, he gives freedom from danger, freedom from animosity, and freedom from oppression to limitless numbers of beings. In giving freedom from danger, freedom from animosity, freedom from oppression to limitless numbers of beings, he gains a share in limitless freedom from danger, freedom from animosity, and freedom from oppression. This is the first gift, the first great gift - original, long-standing, traditional, ancient, unadulterated, unadulterated from the beginning - that is not open to suspicion, will never be open to suspicion, and is unfaulted by knowledgeable contemplatives & Brahmans..."[1]

The following passages Buddha gives us to know how important of the first morality to all living beings:

"All tremble at force,
Of death are all afraid.
Likening others to oneself
Kill not nor cause to kill."[2]

(Sabbe tasanti dandassa
Sabbe bhayanti maccuno
Attanaj upamaj katva
Da haneyya na ghataye)

"Those sages inoffensive
In body ever restrained

---

[1] AN 8.39 - pañca-sila, tr.Thanissaro Bhikkhu

[2] DhP129/Translated from Pali by Ven. Weragoda Sarada Maha Thero

Go unto the Deathless State (Nirvana)
Where gone they grieve no more."[1]

(Ahijsaka ye munayo
Niccaj kayena sajvuta
Te yanti accutaj thanaj
Yattha gantva na socare.)

"Even though adorned, if living in peace
Calm, tamed, established in the holy life,
For beings all laying force aside:
One pure, one peaceful, a bhikkhu is he."[2]

(Alavkato ce pi samaj careyya
Santo danto niyato brahmacari
Sabbesu bhutesu nidhaya dandaj
So brahmano so samano sa bhikkhu.)

"Who blows to beings has renounced
To trembling ones, to bold,
Who causes not to kill nor kills,
That one I call a Brahmin True."[3]

(Nidhaya dandaj bhutesu
Tasesu thavaresu ca
Yo na hanti na ghateti tam
Ahaj brumi brahmanaj.)

The Dalai Lama said, *"I do not see any reason why animals should be slaughtered to serve as human diet when there are so many substitutes. After all, man can live without meat."*

The Buddhist emperor Asoka (268-223 BC) declared in one of his famous Pillar Edicts: *"I have enforced the law against killing certain animals...The greatest progress of*

---

[1] DhP225/Ibid

[2] DhP142/Ibid

[3] DhP405/Ibid

Righteousness among men comes from the exhortation in favor of non-injury to life and abstention from killing living beings."

Mahayana Buddhism upholds the vegetarian way of life. In Mahaparinirvana Sutra: *"The eating of meat extinguishes the seed of great compassion."*

The Lankavatara Sutra says:

"For the sake of love of purity, the bodhisattva should refrain from eating flesh, which is born from semen, blood, etc. For fear of causing terror to living beings let the bodhisattva, who is disciplining himself to attain compassion, refrain from eating flesh...It is not true that meat is proper food and permissible when the animal was not killed by himself, when he did not order others to kill it, when it was not specifically meant for him...Again, there may be some people in the future who...being under the influence of the taste for meat will string together in various ways many sophisticated arguments to defend meat-eating...But...meat-eating in any form, in any manner, and in any place is unconditionally and once and for all prohibited...Meat - eating I have not permitted to anyone, I do not permit, I will not permit..."[1]

In addition to not killing, the Buddha also advised us not to hurt others:

"Whoever harms with force
Those desiring happiness,
As seeker after happiness
One gains no future joy."[2]

Sukhakamani bhutani
Yo dandena vihijsati

---

[1] Lankavatara Sutra, Translated by Daisetz Teitaro Suzuki

[2] DhP131/Translated from Pali by Ven. Weragoda Sarada Maha Thero

Attano sukham esano pecca
So na labhate sukhaj.)

5.2 THE PRECEPT TO REFRAIN FROM TAKING THAT WHICH IS NOT GIVEN

The second one of the five precepts is the 'abandoning taking what is not given (stealing)'. This is the literal translation. That does not mean only abstention from theft, but also implies the rejection of any kind of dishonesty, misappropriation or exploitation, because all of them are the expressions of passionate and selfish desires. [1]

"Who in the world will never take
What is not given, long or short
The great or small, the fair or foul,
That one I call a Brahmin True."[2]

(Yodha dighaj va rassaj va
Anuj thulaj subhasubhaj
Loke adinnaj nadiyati tam
Ahaj brumi brahmanaj.)

"Furthermore, abandoning taking what is not given (stealing), the disciple of the noble ones abstains from taking what is not given. In doing so, he gives freedom from danger, freedom from animosity, freedom from oppression to limitless numbers of beings. In giving freedom from danger, freedom from animosity, freedom from oppression to limitless numbers of beings, he gains a share in limitless freedom from danger, freedom from animosity, and freedom from oppression. This is the second gift..."[3]

---

[1] Bhikkhu. AN 8.39

[2] DhP409/Translated from Pali by Ven. Weragoda Sarada Maha Thero

[3] AN 8.39, tr.Thanissaro Bhikkhu

In positive meaning is not stealing as kike as not making other to be pain, his suffering same mine. When lose something, we are suffering, and as people lose something, they are also too suffering like that. To aware that we do not want to suffer, and do not want others to suffer is a strong sentiment that helping for ourselves to be happy, and help others to be secure; contribute to building a peaceful society and trusting each other. Holding the second precept, whether negative or positive act, this also create the special personality of us, so our good bodily karma could be entirely pure.

Once in Savatthi the Blessed Buddha said this:

"What, householder friends, is the Dhamma explanation befitting to oneself?

Here, householder friends, a Noble Disciple reflects thus: If someone were to take from me, what I have not given, that is, to commit theft, to steal, that would neither be pleasing, nor agreeable to me. If I were to take from whatever kind of another being, what he has not freely given, that is also to commit theft, to steal, and that would neither be pleasing, nor agreeable to that other being either.... What is displeasing and disagreeable to me, is thus also displeasing and disagreeable to any other being too! How can I inflict upon another being, what is displeasing and disagreeable to myself? Having reflected repeatedly thus, then gradually:

1: One will carefully avoid all taking, what is not freely given...

2: One will persuade others also to abstain from all stealing and theft...

3: One will praise only accepting, what is freely and righteously given..."[1]

---

[1] Samyutta Nikaya/tr. Bhikkhu_Samahita

In exactly this way is this good bodily behaviour purified in 3 respects.

The positive matching to the refusal to take what was not given is 'dana' - generosity. In this case, it is also meant not only a sense of generosity and a desire to give, but also very generous action. All those who are in one way or another way connected with the living Buddhist teaching, at least for some time, well aware of what 'dana' is.

"Make haste towards the good
And check the mind for evil.
The one who's is slow to make merit
Delights in the evil mind."[1]

(abhittharetha kalyane
Papa cittaj nivaraye
Dandhaj hi karoto pubbaj
Papasmij ramati mano.)

"Who by wholesome kamma
Covers up the evil done
Illumines the world
As moon when free from clouds."[2]

(yassa papaj kataj kammaj
Kusalena pithiyati
So imaj lokaj pabhaseti
Abbha mutto va candima.)

5.3 THE PRECEPT TO REFRAIN FROM SEXUAL MISCONDUCT

The third one of the five precepts is about 'abandoning illicit sex'. In the sutras, the Buddha explained that the refusal from adultery, as a part of five precepts, is also refusal

---

[1] DhP116/Translated from Pali by Ven. Weragoda Sarada Maha Thero
[2] DhP173/Ibid

of rape and abduction, as these actions are involuntary manifestation of passion and violence both. In cases of rape and abduction, which seems to have been quite common in the relatively loose community of the Buddha's time; violence is committing not only to a certain woman, but to her parents or guardians as well. In the case of adultery, violence exposed the woman's husband, as his family life deliberately destroyed. It should also be noted that in Buddhism marriage is purely a civil contract, not a sacrament. Moreover, the divorce and the monogamy are totally permissible and not mandatory from a religious point of view. In some countries, there are Buddhist communities, in which polygamy is practiced, and that does not consider an 'incorrect sexual behavior'. Moreover, the third precept also includes other different senses, for example, one of them is overindulgence of eating process, which not only encourages the rich and those in power to eat more of what they need, at the expense of those who are deprived of such privileges, - in a global sense; this is causing a catastrophic malnutrition and hunger in the countries of the Third World - but also entails illness, numbness and apathy. Another one example is in satiety of the contemplation of beautiful pictures and hearing - the perception of beautiful sounds, since all pleasures of this kind quickly rise the appearance of attachments and are not conducive to the practice (Thanissaro Bhikkhu).

Its positive matching called 'santustah' (Pali - santutthi) or the contentment. If the person is single, he or she should be content with its celibate state. On the other hand, marriage means to content with your partner who is recognized by surrounding community. In such case, satisfaction is not just the passive acceptance of the existing situation. In terms of modern psychology, it is a positive state of freedom from the need to use sex to satisfy neurotic needs in general and the use of sex to satisfy the neurotic need for change, in particular.

Compliance with rule 'Refraining from committing sexual misconduct', people can obtain the dignity, and freedom from all fears and dangers:

"Furthermore, abandoning illicit sex, the disciple of the noble ones abstains from illicit sex. In doing so, he gives freedom from danger, freedom from animosity, freedom from oppression to limitless numbers of beings. In giving freedom from danger, freedom from animosity, freedom from oppression to limitless numbers of beings, he gains a share in limitless freedom from danger, freedom from animosity, and freedom from oppression. This is the third gift..."[1]

The third moral precept is energy practice of our sex; it's more or less important than the four other precepts. The purpose of this precept is to control ourselves, not engage in unhealthy sexual activity, and to avoid harming ourselves and others.

In most cultures, this is not easily separate the ideas about sex from the idea of sin. There are a lot of strong feelings associated with sex and sexual activity; it may be difficult to think clearly about them. However, we try to leave it aside and look at what the Buddha actually talking about sexual activity.

The Buddha considered the human actions: He taught that every action from our body, speech and mind that create happiness or misery in living. He is not interested in philosophy or opinion for its own interest. He just put the most basic principles; that it is nice and not hurt ourselves or others. If we are honest and careful application of this rule

---

[1] AN 8.39, tr.Thanissaro Bhikkhu

for our actions, we will avoid harming anyone and make the peace and trust each other to our inner world.

> *"Every evil never doing*
> *And in wholesomeness increasing*
> *And one's heart well-purifying:*
> *This is the Buddha's Teaching."*[1]

(Sabbapapassa akaranaj
Kusalassa upasampada
Sacittapariyodapanaj
Etaj buddhana sasanaj.)

In Buddhism, marriage is not a sacrament but a commitment to a specific set of actions. The Buddha did not use the framework to judge marriage and morality. Instead, on his platform is the law of cause and effect (karma), or action. What we've done in the past (or in the past lives) affect our situation now. We also build causality by your current action. If we accept the law of causality as moral model results, the importance is to focus the mind where every action we do: negative actions bring disastrous consequences, and positive actions bring beneficial results for ourselves and others. Noting your intentions and outcomes of our actions from the small things are the most important, just as simple as that.

> *"Think lightly not of evil,*
> *'It will not come to me',*
> *For by the falling of water drops*
> *A water jar is filled.*
> *The fool with evil fills himself,*
> *He soaks up little by little."*[2]

(Mavamabbetha papassa
Na maj taj agamissati

---

[1] DhP183/Translated from Pali by Ven. Weragoda Sarada Maha Thero

[2] DhP121/Ibid

Udabindunipatena
Udakumbho pi purati
Balo purati papassa
Thokathokam pi acinaj.)

A happy couple is actually when sexual activity is an expression of love in a committed relationship. A healthy sex life can bind two persons in love together for many years. It is often a barometer for happy emotions to the partners. It could provide the impetus to melt the unnecessary negative that happens in marriage; a satisfying sex life in open relations and legitimacy can be a reflection of sharing, trust, acceptance, and mutual understanding.

Understanding and accepting in marriage is very necessary to help us completely responsibility for one's family; that is also a best merit. In the Mangala Sutta, the Buddha describes the many ways in which blessings arrive. In this verse, he said doing one's family duty as the gift or blessing:

> *The support of mother and father,*
> *The welfare of spouse and children,*
> *Engaging in unconflicting livelihood;*
> *This is the greatest blessing.*[1]

And what if we don't have an exclusive partner? In modern cultures, sexual experimentation is regarded as a matter of course, and supposed celibacy as an option; this at least would keep us avoiding any major mistakes. But the general rule is that only a partner at a time, and deceit that is not acceptable in relationships. Honesty and trust together are essential in an intimate relationship. Breaking the general principle that is considered immoral behavior in Buddhism:

---

[1] Sn 2.4 tr. John Kelly

"Four things befall that heedless one
Sleeping with one who's wed:
Demerit gained but not good sleep,
Third is blame while fourth is hell."[1]

(Cattari thanani naro pamatto
Apajjati paradarupasevi
Apubbalabhaj nanikamaseyyaj
Nindaj tatiyaj nirayaj catutthaj.)

"Demerit's gained and evil birth,
Scared man and women - brief their joy,
The king decrees a heavy doom:
So none should sleep with one who's wed."[2]

(Apubbalabho ca gati ca papika
Bhitassa bhitaya rati ca thokika
Raja ca dandaj garukaj paneti
Tasma naro paradaraj na seve.)

To keep the precept, the Buddha advised us to be careful to our wrong actions as the following:

"Abandoning misconduct in sensual pleasures, he abstains from misconduct in sensual pleasures; he does not have intercourse with women who are protected by their mother, father, brother, sister, or relatives, who have a husband, who are protected by law, or with those who are garlanded in token of betrothal."[3]

Acts in the field of sexual activity outside partners have painful consequences. It's easy to hurt the feelings for others, and causing hurt feelings for other but even yourself. To avoid hurting yourself and others, the Buddha teaches us to recognize clearly those desires never make us satisfied:

---

[1] DhP309/Translated from Pali by Ven. Weragoda Sarada Maha Thero

[2] DhP310/Ibid

[3] MN41.12. tr. Bhikkhu Ñāṇamoli Bhikkhu Bodhi

"Not by rain of golden coins
Is found desires' satiety,
Desires are dukkha, of little joy,
Thus a wise one understands."[1]

(Na kahapanavassena
Titti kamesu vijjati
Appassada dukkha kama
Iti vibbaya pandito.)

Sex is a kind of illusion, where the nervous system is stimulated by 6 external senses, and thinking craving arises. It is the great illusion which makes us enthralled as we were intrigued by the colored lights on the stage. And the result of the hallucination is touched sexually and continuance of the race as a whole.

"...the interesting thing for us to note is how sex - like everything else - is a purely impersonal force. We tend to think of it in intensely personal terms, but in actual fact it is a force that just flows through us and uses our most wonderful and inspiring emotions for its own ends, which are totally concerned with the continuance of the race as a whole. The idea that it is just a private and wonderful thing between you and me is merely a part of our general illusion. Altogether, it is a prolific breeder of illusions. It can lead a man to think he has found the most wonderful woman in the whole world while everybody else is thinking, 'What on earth can he possibly see in her?'"[2]

When our perception is distorted by the desire for sex, we do not realize its illusions. But the observers, who are not affected by the desire, see it more clearly.

---

[1] DhP186/Translated from Pali by Ven. Weragoda Sarada Maha Thero

[2] Maurice Walshe, *Buddhism and Sex*

"… A Bhikkhu [practitioner] understands mind affected by lust as mind affected by lust, and mind unaffected by lust as mind unaffected by lust."[1]

"Even with pleasures heavenly
That one finds no delight,
The perfect Buddha's pupil
Delights in craving's end."[2]

(Api dibbesu kamesu
Ratij so nadhigacchati
Tanhakkhayarato hoti
Sammasambuddhasavako.)

On the positive side, there are two ways to do with the third precept. Firstly, remember the received precept before we have any behavior action that can lead us into a bad situation which can cause damage. If we are tempted to start an adulterous relationship, think seriously about what would happen after the results of the first meeting and passion. We can imagine an outcome that everyone is happy and no one would be hurt? Such non-sexual relationship can be close and meaning in healthy elements. Secondly, if we extend the idea of sensual energy of mindfulness to include all sources of energy that we exchange with others, view and interact with interactive elements, and contemplation. These are all non-sexual ways to interact with others that can express and build intimacy, trust and love.

Like the four others, this precept is mindfulness' exercise. It is an invitation to observe our actions and motivations more closely, as they just happened.

---

[1] MN10, tr. Bhikkhu Ñāṇamoli Bhikkhu Bodhi

[2] DhP187/Translated from Pali by Ven. Weragoda Sarada Maha Thero

5.4 THE PRECEPT TO REFRAIN FROM INCORRECT

The fourth one of the five precepts is about 'abandoning of lying'. The lie has its roots in the passion, hatred or fear. If you lie, it is either because you want something, or have decided to hurt someone, or because, for whatever reasons, are afraid to tell the truth. Consequently, untruthfulness rooted in unskillful mental state. The positive matching to the refusal of lies is 'Satya' (Pali - sacca), that is to say truthfulness (Thanissaro Bhikkhu).

However, every day, for work and the communication we have hundreds of choices at the same time: is to lie or tell the truth, which often occurs whitout thinking, and we ignore deeply impact of the decisions that do not seem important. Even the smallest lie can affect health, affect relationships, and influence our choices. Conversely, honesty brings amazingly psychological benefits. Here is the way the truth and the lie affects the brain and our health every day.

'Anita Kelly and Lijuan Wang of Notre Dame has recruited a group of 110 people from aged 18-71 years old, and told them that once a week for ten weeks they must comein to lie detector machine, then report how many times in last week they had lied. But the group was divided into two. 55 of them received clearly instructions in how to avoid lying. (They may avoid telling the truth, or did not answer, just outside the conversation.) The other group had no guides, only require to come in once per week and tell the truth about how many times they had lied previous week.

As a result, everyone lied less. However, the group has received advice on how to avoid lying reduced their significantly. And in questionnaires, those who had lied less had better reporting of mental and physical health. They reported improvements in their relationships, well sleep, less stress, less headaches, and fewer sore throats.'

We should know that stress harms our brain and body in many terrible ways. Lying contributes to our stress level and when we do this several times a day, we need to consider the impact of our secrets. The harm is not obvious; it is easy to influence numerous health issues we encounter in our everyday life.

Abandoning of lying means that no immoral behavior, causing a dangerous enemy for oneself, others, and living beings, and obstructing the freedom and happiness of oneself and others:

"Furthermore, abandoning lying, the disciple of the noble ones abstains from lying. In doing so, he gives freedom from danger, freedom from animosity, freedom from oppression to limitless numbers of beings. In giving freedom from danger, freedom from animosity, freedom from oppression to limitless numbers of beings, he gains a share in limitless freedom from danger, freedom from animosity, and freedom from oppression. This is the fourth gift..."[1]

Moreover, life is no fixed framework. Lying causes stress and other terrible problems; it is useful and even necessary at a certain time. When our safety or honesty getting in danger, we probably should not choose the truth; here called means for ourselves and others, unless exceptions always exist. And regardless how our intentions, lying makes us becoming persons who do not feel confident and comfortable. Generally, honesty gives more benefits for mental and physical health than dishonesty. However, we are the complex creatures, so we make complex decisions in every day. We'll find a reason to lie because it is essential to preserve the dignity or politeness. But think about the long term effects and the lying will defend us or others in a specific time. We cannot

---

[1] AN 8.39, tr.Thanissaro Bhikkhu

always tell the truth, but makes your body and mind to be happy, and avoid hurting other people as possible.

To avoid causing suffering for oneself and others, the Buddha proposed four principles of speech to prevent speach immoral potentially harming others. The four methods of not lying make us becoming noble and more reliable ones:

"This is how one is made pure in four ways by verbal action."

1. *"There is the case where a certain person, abandoning false speech, abstains from false speech. When he has been called to a town meeting, a group meeting, a gathering of his relatives, his guild, or of the royalty, if he is asked as a witness, 'Come & tell, good man, what you know': If he doesn't know, he says, 'I don't know.' If he does know, he says, 'I know.' If he hasn't seen, he says, 'I haven't seen.' If he has seen, he says, 'I have seen.' Thus he doesn't consciously tell a lie for his own sake, for the sake of another, or for the sake of any reward. Abandoning false speech, he abstains from false speech. He speaks the truth, holds to the truth, and is firm, reliable, no deceiver of the world."*[1]

According the paragraph above, initially the Buddha wanted to advise us not to lie, to say the truth, and create confidence for not defraud others. Indeed people only believe you when you say things no secrets, no lies, and telling what you saw. Denying the truth is bad karma, close to death in the belief of the relationships, the death of conscience.

> *"With one denying truth there goes to hell*
> *That one who having done says 'I did not'.*
> *Both of them are making kammas base*
> *Are equal after death."*[2]

[1] AN 10.176 Cunda Kammaraputta Sutta: To Cunda the Silversmith, translated from the Pali by Thanissaro Bhikkhu

[2] DhP306/Translated from Pali by Ven. Weragoda Sarada Maha Thero

(Abhutavadi nirayaj upeti
Yo va pi katva na karomi ti caha
Ubho pi pecca sama bhavanti
Nihinakamma manuja parattha.)

2. *"Abandoning divisive speech he abstains from divisive speech. What he has heard here he does not tell there to break those people apart from these people here. What he has heard there he does not tell here to break these people apart from those people there. Thus reconciling those who have broken apart or cementing those who are united, he loves concord, delights in concord, enjoys concord, and speaks things that create concord."*[1]

Our society is more fractured for divisive words; the words that make for cultura, race, and religion divide... make prolonged tonggue wars. We have a habit of saying things which don't bring benefits to both parties but just for ourselves in the relationship, or the other partners. On other side, verbal fleer, the media reported one-dimensional, and the spokesman divisive created hatred has contributed to the current social violences that the innocent persons must suffer in doubt just because a disruptive speech, not constructive word, and do not build up belief in love for each other. Instead divisive speech, we should say in constructive practice, so the relationships will change in a positive direction.

"Who utters speech instructive
True and gentle too
Who gives offence to none
That one I call a Brahmin True."[2]

---

[1] AN 10.176 Cunda Kammaraputta Sutta, translated from the Pali by Thanissaro Bhikkhu

[2] DhP408/Translated from Pali by Ven. Weragoda Sarada Maha Thero

(Akakkasaj vibbapanij
Giraj saccam udiraye
Yaya nabhisaje kabci tam
Ahaj brumi brahmanaj.)

3. *"Abandoning abusive speech, he abstains from abusive speech. He speaks words that are soothing to the ear, that are affectionate, that go to the heart, that are polite, appealing & pleasing to people at large."*[1]

In this third part, we should know about the abusive words in relationships and communication. The abusive speech is saying insults, as obscene words, curse words, defamatory words ... for others, and taking of the reputation of people; or say something which are not conducive to someone, and spreading misinformation to demeaning others... Before talking, we should consider our words are the insulting words or not; we need to do a self-test by our cognitive ability to abusive speech. Sometimes what we see from others, that reflect on what we have done for them. Verbal venom from bad words have unpredictable infection; it spreads like the growth of tumors and difficult to treat.

Verbal brutality and insult's very strong to break in relationships, marriage, friends and partners. To stop the risk from evil words, before saying we should consider carefully is these words torment us and others? May these bring love and joy to oneself and others? So we would not be abused by ourselves and also not hurt either.

"Speak not harshly to other folk,
Speaking so, they may retort.
Dukkha indeed is quarrelsome speech
And force for force may hurt you."[2]

---

[1] AN 10.176, Cunda Kammaraputta Sutta

[2] DhP133/Translated from Pali by Ven. Weragoda Sarada Maha Thero

(Mavoca pharusaj kabci
Vutta pativadeyyu taj
Dukkha hi sarambhakatha
Patidanda phuseyyu taj.)

4. *"Abandoning idle chatter, he abstains from idle chatter. He speaks in season, speaks what is factual, what is in accordance with the goal, the Dhamma, & the Vinaya. He speaks words worth treasuring, seasonable, reasonable, circumscribed, and connected with the goal."* [1]

Idle chatter-gossip is to say polished, crap, and nonsense while leisurely time. Speech has no goals, ideals or depth in communication, that is not worth; these words just incurred negativity in our minds and others. Usually, the lay Buddhists get many needs to speak in their spare time, such as talking about the family, friends, and jobs ... But Buddha advised that the embroidered words, the idle talking should restrain and restrict as much as possible, because the words are no practical benefit, and likely to cause disturbance of our mind. In the case of idle, try to avoid meaningless words and no the human values while communicating. Need to aim of the teachings in words, thus the suffering can be eliminated, wholesome and wisdom just develop as well as, and yourself and others are attained practical benefits.

"For one who falsely speaks,
Who disregards the Dhamma,
Who denies other lives:
No evil this one will not do." [2]

(Ekaj dhammaj atitassa
Musavadissa jantuno
Vitinnaparalokassa natthi papaj akariyaj.)

---

[1] AN 10.176, Cunda Kammaraputta Sutta

[2] DhP176/Translated from Pali by Ven. Weragoda Sarada Maha Thero

For those who are ordained, the Buddha's advice not to discuss or debate in any secular thing, just focus the ideal of liberation.

> *"If like a broken gong*
> *Never you reverberate,*
> *Quarrelling's not part of you,*
> *That Nibbana's reached."*[1]

> (Sace n'eresi attanaj
> Kajso upahato yatha
> Esa patto'si nibbanaj
> Sarambho te na vijjati.)

In short, to undertake the training to refrain from false speech, the Buddha advised us to control our speech by the 5 ways following to know what should be said and what shouldn't:

"And what other five conditions must be established in himself?

[1] "Do I speak at the right time, or not?

[2] "Do I speak of facts, or not?

[3] "Do I speak gently or harshly?

[4] "Do I speak profitable words or not?

[5] "Do I speak with a kindly heart, or inwardly malicious?

"O Bhikkhus, these five conditions are established in himself by a bhikkhu who desires to admonish another."[2]

---

[1] DhP 134/Ibid

[2] AN V, from the Patimokkha, Ñanamoli Thera, trans.

5.5 THE PRECEPT TO REFRAIN FROM INTOXICATING DRINKS AND DRUGS WHICH LEAD TO CARELESSNESS

And the last one of the five precepts is the 'abandoning the use of intoxicants' which cause loss of consciousness. This means some kind of rejection of such things like alcohol and drugs. However, there are some differences in the interpretations of these instructions. In some Buddhist countries its interpretation means demand of absolute sobriety, in the other ones it means just a call to some kind of moderation in the usage of things, which, in case of being taken in large doses, cause intoxication. Everyone is free to make a choice between these two interpretations. [1]

The intoxicants such as alcohol, cocaine and heroin cause heedlessness (pamada), so that affects badly others around us - without the ability to see the results our actions. Getting drunk is a deliberate way to make us in situation of unawareness. The fifth precept is observation instructions to causes and impact of consumer behavior on alcohol, and addictions as drugs, so to help the lay Buddhists towards a healthy action. Alcohol and drugs are the most obvious cause of the chronic heedlessness, lack of ethics and liability, uncontrollable desire, no sense of shame, not realizing what true and false in action and easy provoked, and even murder.

Drunk is not a part of Buddhist culture although it seems to have become a common phenomenon in modern society. The consumption of alcohol was prevalent before and during the time of Buddha, but he never approved it in the practice. Really, today is something that's often practiced not necessarily meaning that it completes good and healthy. Proponents of beer and alcohol are a factor to

---

[1] AN 8.39, Thanissaro Bhikkhu

promote friendships and partnerships, but they forget factly that many friendships have drowned in these intoxicants. The quarrels, conflicts and unruly behavior often stems from the consumption of alcoholic beverages that represent clear evidence of their ignoble state under the influence of intoxicants. Friendships just are set basing on compassion and mutual understanding rather than on beer, wine, or alcohol. Drinking alcohol only create an atmosphere of general excitement of those who drinking together (and can be a nuisance for those who do not drink), but it never was a necessary condition for interpersonal relations. Usually, people use alcohol as an excuse to be drunk. According to the statistics of family and social instability, the rate of divorce, domestic and traffic accidents, violence and crime always increases with the drinking and drug addiction. In addition, drunker' physical conditions are still being warned by the health experts. (https://www.niaaa.nih.gov/alcohol-health/).

The Buddha described addiction to intoxicants is one of six causes of break down. And it leads to six major drawbacks: loss of wealth, disputes and conflicts, poverty and disease, causing of shame, shameless behavior and indecent, and undermine intelligence and mental abilities. He has also given his own rules to avoid the using of intoxicating substances because they are the cause of heedlessness (pamada). The heedlessness means a state of disorder, lack of moral status, and undistinguishable right or wrong things. It is status of the lost of transparency, heedfulness, mindfulness (appamada), and the basic moral elements base on acutely awareness of the dangers of immoral status...

"Furthermore, abandoning the use of intoxicants, the disciple of the noble ones abstains from taking intoxicants. In doing so, he gives freedom from danger, freedom from animosity, freedom from oppression to limitless numbers of beings. In giving freedom from danger, freedom from animosity, freedom from oppression to limitless numbers of beings, he gains a share in limitless freedom from danger, freedom from animosity, and freedom from oppression. This is the fifth gift, the fifth great gift..."[1]

However, in cultural society, alcohol restraint is not an admired characteristic to the consumer culture of our orientation. It may be an uphill battle, but its rewards are very great. The results can be surprising. If one observes the fact the meticulous honesty, one was found that the lust feelings just come and go; if one committed to abstinence, one would have real freedom with oneself without accompanying with crowd! Restraint is not repression, but declared independence from unwholesome states. It is choosing something more lasting value than temporary pleasures and superficiality. The happiest people are those who live a simplest way; they are less worried, because they do not create problems for themselves or others. They know that their living arrangements surrounding exquisite food consumption, entertainment, and intoxicants cannot meet what they necessary. Practicing precepts, the lay Buddhists live happy and healthy life, and also can bring the best things for themselves and others. Those who obey to this precept will achieve a sense of security, calm and confidence, and help them to pursue the best path as possible as.

> *"Or has distilled, fermented drinks:*
> *Who with abandon follows these*
> *Extirpates the root of self*
> *Even here in this very world."[2]*

(Suramerayapanaj ca yo
Naro anuyubjati

---

[1] AN 8.39, tr.Thanissaro Bhikkhu

[2] DhP247/Translated from Pali by Ven. Weragoda Sarada Maha Thero

Idhevameso lokasmij
Mulaj khanati attano.)

Positive compliance of this instruction - 'smriti' (Pali - sati)/attention or awareness is an effective criterion. If you are able to drink alcohol without losing care (this is possible), then drink. But if you cannot perform, then refrain. However, you should be very honest with yourself and do not pretend that you are careful and realize at the time, when you are just drunk. Thus, while the fifth instruction is interpreted as a moderate thing, but on the basis of its positive compliance, in most cases require complete abstinence.

With the major five precepts the Buddha taught, in my opinion, there could not be any questions about of how this precepts could help humanity nowadays. Just imagine how quickly could be the humanity develop without applying the five precepts. Without resorting to such methods, not because they are prohibited by law, but because of their own personal humanistic motives. Nevertheless, we should not forget that the adoption of certain perception, as if it was not desirable, you never should need to highlight it, for each of the commandments is inherently important and the attainment of freedom or nirvana is possible just for those who follow that path until the end. At the same time, if will take a more realistic look at the modern world of today, we can easily understand that society is still very far from the general adoption of the Buddha's teachings. Seemingly, it will benefit everyone living on the planet, yet we should not expect the adoption of these things at the legislative level, because the people in whose hands power is will try to stop this, because of their egoistic desires and fears. Thus, the only way for humankind to approach as close as possible to the Buddhism is trying to follow these precepts as hard as possible, always starting with ourselves.

As we mentioned before, besides 'five precepts' there are also 'eight precepts' and 'ten precepts' as well. The difference between five and eight composed in that fact that 'eight precepts' is more advanced 'five', as they imply not just the instruction for moral behavior, but instructions for leading more ascetic life by practicing this techniques to follow the Buddha's way more strictly. They are the following:

1. 'abandoning the taking of life - abstain from the taking of life'

2. 'abandoning the taking of what is not given - abstain from taking what is not given'

3. 'abandoning uncelibacy - live a celibate life, aloof, refraining from the sexual act that is the villager's way'

4. 'abandoning false speech - abstain from false speech'

5. 'abandoning fermented & distilled liquors that cause heedlessness - abstain from fermented & distilled liquors that cause heedlessness'

6. 'live on one meal a day, abstaining from food at night, refraining from food at the wrong time of day' (that means from noon until dawn)

7. 'abstain from dancing, singing, music, watching shows, wearing garlands, beautifying themselves with perfumes & cosmetics'

8. 'abandoning high & imposing seats & beds - abstain from high & imposing seats & beds'

Thus we see that 'eight precepts' are the training rules for the people who chose harder but in some kind shorter way, who can afford themselves devoting much more of their time the Buddha's way. The beginners observing this rules during periods of intensive meditation and, of course, during the days of 'Uposatha' which is the day of observance for every Buddhist, as the Buddha told, the day for 'cleaning of the defiled mind through the proper technique'. The 'eight precepts' is one of those proper techniques, according to him. As it seen, the eight precepts are much more difficult to complete and require more efforts to achieve, relatively to five.[1]

In addition to the eight precepts for lay Buddhists to practice, 'Ten precepts' were created for novice monks; they are usually written or spoken as a some kind of sacrament, also here they are:

1. 'I undertake the precept to refrain from destroying living creatures.'
2. 'I undertake the precept to refrain from taking that which is not given.'
3. 'I undertake the precept to refrain from sexual activity.'
4. 'I undertake the precept to refrain from incorrect speech.'
5. 'I undertake the precept to refrain from intoxicating drinks and drugs which lead to carelessness.'
6. 'I undertake the precept to refrain from eating at the forbidden time (i.e., after noon).'
7. 'I undertake the precept to refrain from dancing, singing, music, going to see entertainments.'
8. 'I undertake the precept to refrain from wearing garlands, using perfumes, and beautifying the body with cosmetics.'
9. 'I undertake the precept to refrain from lying on a high or luxurious sleeping place.'
10. 'I undertake the precept to refrain from accepting gold and silver (money).' (The Buddhist Monastic Code)

---

[1] AN 3.70, Thanissaro Bhikkhu

As it seen above, they are almost similar to eight precepts, except two differences: the seventh rule was divided for two in order to avoid incorrect interpretations, and, in addition, the last one rule, which forbids the handling of money, was added. We may find that ten moral principles can be divided into three categories. In the first category - three bodily actions followed by the category of speech acts which we will not only refrain from untrue speech, but also from slander, harsh words and unwanted speech; all this in order to help us to be vigilant with regard to our speech. And finally, to keep our mind, there is a mental action: to refrain from greed, from frustration and from the untrue beliefs. And making pure of body, speech and mind through the compliance these precepts is what Buddha praised as follows:

> *"Assiduous and mindful,*
> *Pure kamma making, considerate,*
> *Restrained, by Dhamma heedful living,*
> *For one such spread renown."*[1]

> (Uṭṭhānavato satīmato
> Sucikammassa nisammakārino
> Saññatassa dhammajīvino
> Appamattassa yasobhivaḍḍhati.)

> *"By energy and heedfulness,*
> *By taming and by self-control,*
> *The one who's wise should make as isle*
> *No flood can overwhelm."*[2]

> (Uṭṭhānen' appamādena
> Saṃyamena damena ca
> Dīpaṃ kayirātha medhāvī
> Yaṃ ogho n'ābhikīrati.)

---

[1] DhP24/Translated by Ven. Weragoda Sarada Maha Thero

[2] DhP25/Ibid

6. THE EIGHTFOLD PATH AS A WAY OF DEVELOPMENT OF WISDOM AND ETHICS IN THE SOCIETY

The Noble Eightfold Path (八正道-āryāstāngika-mārgaalso/known as the "Middle Way") is one of the foundations of the whole Buddha's teaching. The Buddha described it as the way which leads to the cessation of suffering (dukkha) and the achievement of self-awakening. This path is needed to develop the insight into the true nature of all things (or reality), and for the destruction of craving, hatred and ignorance, which are the so-called 'three roots of vice' or 'three poisons', which are present in the mind of every unenlightened being. The Noble Eightfold Path is what the Fourth Noble Truth of which the Buddha tells us, and at the same time, the understanding of the Four Noble Truths is the first element of this Path.

All elements or steps, stages of the Path begin with the word 'right', which in the Pali language sounds like 'samma'. For a greater precision, discipline and cohesion it can also be noted as this word also means 'ideal' or 'perfect'. In Buddhist symbolism, the Noble Eightfold Path is usually imagined in the form of the 'Wheel of Dhamma' in which eight spokes represent the eight elements of the path. According to ancient Sutras of the Pali Canon, the Noble Eightfold Path was rediscovered by Gautama Buddha in his quest for enlightenment.

"In the same way I saw an ancient path, an ancient road, traveled by the Rightly Self-awakened Ones of former times. And what is that ancient path, that ancient road, traveled by the Rightly Self-awakened Ones of former times? Just this noble eightfold path: right view, right aspiration, right speech, right action, right livelihood, right effort, right mindfulness, and right concentration. That is the ancient path, the ancient road, traveled by the Rightly Self-awakened Ones of former times. I followed that path. Following it, I came to direct knowledge of aging & death, direct knowledge of the origination of aging & death, and direct knowledge of the cessation of aging & death, direct knowledge of the path leading to the cessation of aging & death. I followed that path. Following it, I came to direct knowledge of birth... becoming... clinging... craving... feeling... contact... the six sense media... name-&-form... consciousness, direct knowledge of the origination of consciousness, direct knowledge of the cessation of consciousness, and direct knowledge of the path leading to the cessation of consciousness. I followed that path"[1] (Bhikkhu, SN 12.65).

Although Eightfold Path referred to the steps on a path, is not meat that a sequential process of practice, but the eight aspects of life; all of which are contained in our thought and behavior, and in everyday life. Therefore, the circumstances shall be improved in order to move closer to the Buddhist path.

In Buddhism, the Eightfold Path is not the moral rules in arbitrary or passing down orders from superiors; it is meant as a guide to consider, to contemplate, and be applied only if each step are shown entirely as a part of life that we are seeking. Buddhism never mentions blind faith; it seeks to promote the research and process of discovery ourselves.

The texts describe Eight methods have been followed and practiced by all the previous Buddhas. The Eightfold Path leads people self-awakening and liberation from suffering (dukkha) of three evils and thought disorder. The Buddha taught this method to his disciples, and they can pass on it

---

[1] SN 12.65, Thanissaro Bhikkhu

to others for the purpose self-enlightenment and salvation while helping others.

"Following it, I came to direct knowledge of fabrications, direct knowledge of the origination of fabrications, direct knowledge of the cessation of fabrications, and direct knowledge of the path leading to the cessation of fabrications. Knowing that directly, I have revealed it to monks, nuns, male lay followers and female lay followers, so that this holy life has become powerful, rich, detailed, well-populated, wide-spread, proclaimed among celestial & human beings."[1]

Next, we are going to analyze each element of the Eighfold Path in details, because each of it is extremely important for a whole Buddhist teaching.

6.1 RIGHT VIEW *(samyak-dṛṣṭi / sammā-diṭṭhi)*

The first point of the Eightfold Path is the 'right view', which is also called 'right vision' or 'perfect vision', as it usually translated from original language (samyak-dṛṣṭi / sammā-diṭṭhi). However, we shall notice that this is not an accurate translation. So the 'right' in such case, means either 'perfect', 'proper', 'whole', than the opposite word to 'wrong'.

So what is Right View? It is indisputable that this is a first stage of the Noble Eightfold Path of the Buddha. As mentioned above, the eight stages of the path are divided into three groups, and the Right View is an element of the first group - Wisdom (Sanskrit: prajñā, Pāli: paññā). This is the most important step, because from it, and only from it, begins the following of the path of the Buddha. Many people believe that Right View means to study all the theoretical Buddhism base, they think that the first step implies a complete

---

[1] Ibid...

investigation and a logical interpretation of the Buddha's teachings; however, it is not so, because its definition by the Buddha sounds as following: "There is what is given, what is offered, what is sacrificed. There are fruits & results of good & bad actions. There is this world & the next world. There is mother & father. There are spontaneously reborn beings; there are contemplatives & Brahmans who, faring rightly & practicing rightly, proclaim this world & the next after having directly known & realized it for themselves."[1]

That demonstrates to us that Right View lies rather in a sphere of emotional experiences than in the field of understanding with the help of intelligence is a complete understanding. In its essence, Right View is a spiritual insight, experience, and having gone through that person comes to his or her own path. Without overcoming it and assimilating this experience, it is impossible to advance further since all further steps are based, in fact, solely on the Right View. If in the future a person, depending on their personal situation may follow the path in a free manner, for example, the first sequence may revise its methods of earning a living (the fifth stage), and then work on their own speech (the third stage, respectively), so it does not have practical difference. Nevertheless, without the Right View, following eightfold path is impossible. Thus, Right View is a harbinger of following Eightfold Path.

Right View includes Worldly right view and Out-of-worldly right view. The Worldly right view is the establishment of concepts of good and evil, cause and effect, karma, and laity and saint ... It also known as self-karma' right view, so we understand about our own good and evil actions that are received by ourselves. Having the Right View, we can clearly

---

[1] Geoffrey DeGraff, Wings to Awakening, pass.106

define what good and what bad karma is, and the root of moral and immoral.

However, self-karma' right view is not the way to approach towards liberation; full understanding the Four Noble Truths that is complete demand for Out-of-worldly right view. Four Noble Truths Right of the Out-of-worldly right view has two stages of development: One is the Right view of depending upon the truth (saccānulomika-sammādiṭṭhi 諦隨順見), as corresponds to the Four Noble Truth's wise, and received principles to dharma of the Four noble Truth; that is the concept of the nature Right view. Other one is to contemplate the truth of Righ view (saccapaṭivedha-sammādiṭṭhi 諦通達見) which is wisdom arising by practice Four Noble Truth, and that is experience of Right view. Eightfold Path is the initial penetration in nature of the Four Noble Truth, so whatever ones have deep insigh the Four Noble they are attained Nirvana. Therefore, the Four Noble Truth is the first point and also last point of the path of liberation. The Right view is also wise eyes - to see clearly the nature of the three poisons of greed, hatred and ignorance, and be freed from them by right looking with the phenomenon principles of impermanence and non-self.

According to Sangharakshita, in the Indian Buddhist tradition, Eightfold Path can be divided in two parts: the 'Path of Vision' (darsana-marga), which includes the right view, and the 'Path of Transformation' (bhavana-marga), including remaining seven steps. [1]

Right View is primarily the vision of the whole nature of being: a vision of the ways of conditioned being, as well as the vision of the unconditioned and the ways to achieve it in the context of Buddhism: "...Kaccayana, this world is in

---

[1] Sangharakshita, The Buddha's Noble Eightfold Path, p.17

bondage to attachments, clingings (sustenances), & biases. But one such as this does not get involved with or cling to these attachments, clingings, fixations of awareness, biases, or obsessions, nor is he resolved on 'my self'; he has no uncertainty or doubt that, when there is arising, only stress is arising, and that when there is passing away, only stress is passing away. In this, one's knowledge is independent of others. It is to this extent, Kaccayana, that there is right view."[1] Therefore, Right View implies a proper understanding of one or another thing, and in the first place it is related to the Four Noble Truths-the characteristics of the conditioned being-karma and rebirth.

The real value of the Right View principle is not easy to describe in words, but rather thought a special spiritual experience, which naturally occurs only in special circumstances, or in the special practices. Since it is highly personal recommended, every individual may experience it in different ways. Some people come to Right View, having experienced some personal tragedy, by which they decide to consider the principles of being more intensively, trying to get to the meaning of life. Others may have come up to this level, due to ecstatic feeling, which came from the contemplations of nature, or from listening to music. Some have come to that in a long meditation, constantly keeping their minds in a pure tranquility. Sometimes, understanding of Right View is attained with age, when a person is already having some experience on the basis of his view of the world, and by comparing the set of facts finally sees a glimpse of truth, and the future direction, which is to follow.[2] This is illustrated, for example, by the following quote of the Buddha: "And what is right view? Knowledge with regard to stress, knowledge

---

[1] SN 12.15, Kaccayanagotta Sutta

[2] Sangharakshita, The Buddha's Noble Eightfold Path, p.18-20

with regard to the origination of stress, knowledge with regard to the cessation of stress, knowledge with regard to the way of practice leading to the cessation of stress: This is called right view[1] which shows the possibility of coming to the Right View through the interaction with stress.

As it was mentioned above, everything that was spoken by the Buddha is not a strict directive to act specifically. The Buddha merely gave a good advice to the mankind, gave the direction where to go and what to strive for, and gave the map while not denying the fact that there is possibility of existence of parallel roads leading to nirvana. In our opinion, the existence of such parallel paths is a good proof of the effectiveness of the method: if different people came to the same conclusions and acquired a similar view of the world, or in other words, if different opinions and theories, eventually led to similar conclusions, not denying, but only proving it, then we can say that the theory is confirmed experimentally. In many systems, there is the concept of beliefs, there is a concept of a starting point, which is often very similar or completely identical to the 'mystical experience', as it is commonly called.

For example, let us take a look at newer theories and concepts of personal development, which entered the world recently. A famous American psychologist Timothy Leary (October 1920 - May 1996), promotes the concept of 'eight-circuit model of consciousness' of his own authorship, and also speaks of a certain education, which is the starting point for the further personal development. In his concept he describes eight circuits operating in the human mind, with four of them at this stage of human development, are given to us initially, which means that each person on the planet has

---

[1] DN 22, Maha-satipatthana Sutta: The Great Frames of Reference

these circuits from birth. The remaining four are given not to everyone and the purpose of existence; following this theory, it consists in their further development. To open a fifth stage, it is required 'to realize the world' that often occurs through a 'mystical experience'. In his book Neurologic, Leary calls such condition 'the rapture circuit' (Leary, V - I). As methods for achieving such a state Leary, among other things, points out a long-term practice of meditation. His associate in a worldview, Robert Anton Wilson, in his book Prometheus Rising also refers to many mystics of the past, such as Aleister Crowley and Gurdjieff who said similar things by other names.

However, basis of Right View in Buddhism is also correctly understanding about skillfulness and unskillfulness, about what should do and should not do, as the actions bring benefits to one and others that is illuminated by the Right View, so the actions are not being driven by greed, hatred, delusion, arrogance…And those who have Right view in Buddhism are likely to escape the suffering, and afflictions, and achieved joy-happiness right here and now:

"…Right view is…When a disciple of the noble ones discerns what is unskillful, discerns the root of what is unskillful, discerns what is skillful, and discerns the root of what is skillful, it is to that extent that he is a person of right view, one whose view is made straight, who is endowed with verified confidence in the Dhamma, and who has arrived at this true Dhamma.

Now what is unskillful? Taking life is unskillful, taking what is not given… sexual misconduct… lying… abusive speech… divisive tale-bearing… idle chatter is unskillful. Covetousness… ill will… wrong views are unskillful. These things are termed unskillful.

And what are the roots of what is unskillful? Greed is a root of what is unskillful; aversion is a root of what is unskillful; delusion is a root of what is unskillful. These are termed the roots of what is unskillful.

And what is skillful? Abstaining from taking life is skillful, abstaining from taking what is not given... from sexual misconduct... from lying... from abusive speech... from divisive tale-bearing... abstaining from idle chatter is skillful. Lack of covetousness... lack of ill will... right views are skillful. These things are termed skillful.

And what are the roots of what is skillful? Lack of greed is a root of what is skillful, lack of aversion is a root of what is skillful, and lack of delusion is a root of what is skillful. These are termed the roots of what is skillful.

When a disciple of the noble ones discerns what is unskillful in this way, discerns the root of what is unskillful in this way, discerns what is skillful in this way, and discerns the root of what is skillful in this way, when - having entirely abandoned passion-obsession, having abolished aversion-obsession, having uprooted the view-&-conceit obsession 'I am', having abandoned ignorance & given rise to clear knowing - he has put an end to suffering & stress right in the here-&-now, it is to this extent that a disciple of the noble ones is a person of right view, one whose view is made straight, who is endowed with verified confidence in the Dharma, and who has arrived at this true Dhamma."[1]

Deeply, the Right View is the view of dependent origination or dependent arising (Sanskrit: pratītyasamutpāda; Pali: paṭiccasamuppāda), states that all dharmas (phenomena). It means understanding things all belong functioning of dependent and interdependence, nothing exists

---

[1] MN 9, Sammaditthi Sutta - Thanissaro Bhikkhu translated

independently. Buddha said: "One who sees the Dhamma, sees Dependent Origination." (Majjhima Nikya). Thus Dharma is also dependent arising: all dharmas ("things") arise in dependence upon other dharmas; which illustrated by explains following:

"When there is this, that comes to be;
With the arising of this, that arises.
When there is not this, that does not come to be;
With the cessation of this, that ceases."

(Majjhima Nikaya)

Understanding dependent arising is the key to liberation, and is also aware of the reality in true nature to the enlightened; that is to see the things correlation exists, or the essences of dharma is selflessness or anatta. In this angle, the Right View is out of ignorance, craving and clinging - cause of rebirth suffering (dukkha) to all beings.

The Right view of dependent origination is also the view of Middle Way; it means avoiding the extreme of indulgence in pleasures of the senses and the extreme of self-mortification. The Middle Way is the extent between this and that, between extremes of eternalism and nihilism…in a state of harmony moderation and neutral to have peace really.

In Buddhism, having Right view that, we cannot be driven by delusions which maked us propelling into the endless pains, thus also realizing the value of perfect peace in our heart.

6.2. RIGHT RESOLVE (samyak-saṃkalpa / sammā sankappa)

The second part of the Noble Eightfold Path is the 'right resolve' (samyak-saṃkalpa / sammā sankappa), which is also known as 'right intention', 'perfect emotion' and under several other names. The fact is that word 'saṃkalpa' means 'will', thus, it is would be wrong to interpret 'samyak-saṃkalpa' for limited with meaning of Right Resolve.

It would be more proper to call this principle the 'Perfect Will' or 'Integral Emotion', since it is in accordance of volutional and sensual side of human nature with Right View. Right Resolve knowingly takes the second place: it is, in some way, a link between Right View and the rest of six stages. In addition, basing on the division of the Eightfold Path to the 'Path of Vision' and the 'Path of Transformation', which was discussed above, Right Resolve is the first stage of the path of transformation. Of course, this is not accidental: 'samyak-saṃkalpa' teaches us how to transform our will and our emotional responses in accordance with Right View, because as we know, any belief and any aspiration should be supported by the respective emotions. "And what is right resolve? Being resolved on renunciation, on freedom from ill-will, on harmlessness: This is called right resolve."[1]

The 'right resolve' could be divided into two aspects, the first one of which is 'The Negative Aspect of Perfect Emotion'. It includes three concepts: 'naiskramya' - lack of desire, 'avyapada' - lack of hatred, and 'avihimsa' - lack of cruelty. Each of those elements is highly important.

Thus, 'naiskramya' implies rejection of greed, for a cleaner view of the world. This is particularly true in today's world, where people cannot imagine a normal life without certain things (such as a mobile phone, computer, car and so on). The whole capitalism system is built on continuous production and satisfaction of wishes, passions and desires. More and more new products and services on a daily basis appear in the market and catch us in the eye, in fact, using the latest advertising technologies, manufacturers try to

---

[1] SN 45.8, Thanissaro Bhikkhu

awaken in us the desire to possess those or other things that; if we think about it, we do not need at all too much. On the contrary, as we have seen, all these desires only throw us farther and farther away on our path to Enlightenment. With the development of progress, desires are imposed on us from our childhood, and this affects all layers of the population in all countries of the world. Of course, the temptations to different desires have taken place at all times; however, it is unlikely they were so sophisticated and pervasive as it is now.

The second point -- 'avyapada' - implies the absence of hatred and anger. It is very closely linked to the previous one, although it is not always visible at first sight. In most cases, the foundation for anger is an unfulfilled desire. In vain dreaming about something, we can be unjustly angry with anyone, then imagining him or her to be guilty of our own failures. Another outcome of unfulfilled desires is envy. In history, there are many examples when people succumbing to these and similar emotions, have caused enormous damage both to others and themselves, and the amount of this damage was dependent only on the amount of power they possessed. We should note that negative aspects are tightly interconnected, and basically each of them is a consequence of another one. Therefore, if a man is mean, he is, probably, greedy as well, and vice versa: "There is the case where a certain person is not covetous. He does not covet the belongings of others, thinking, 'Oh, that what belongs to others would be mine!' He bears no ill will and is not corrupt in the resolves of his heart. (He thinks) 'May these beings be free from animosity, free from oppression, free from trouble, and maybe they look after themselves with ease!"[1]

The last term of the 'The Negative Aspect of Perfect Emotion', as we have already said, is 'avihimsa'. Cruelty is

---

[1] AN 10.176, Cunda Kammaraputta Sutta

usually worse than simple malice, since it implies the infliction of pain to other beings. Causing pain and suffering to other beings, violent people enjoy the process, which is against nature. However, often the cruelty can occur unconsciously because of stupidity or misunderstanding. In today's world, thanks to the advent of television and the Internet, from childhood our mind is under constant pressure. In particular, many children saw the news on television or were watching the cartoons, trying to emulate the heroes of these episodes in their games, so the level of violence of which often is much higher than normal. Thus, from the very childhood each of us is instilled more with a more lenient attitude to this phenomenon than it should be. And, of course, people do not always see this problem allowing the vices of others to evolve. Thus, what once were only childish funny games, and later can develop into a more pernicious passion in the adulthood.

The second aspect of the 'right resolve' is 'The Positive Aspect of Perfect Emotion', includes positive matches of the 'naiskramya', 'avyapada', and 'avihimsa', which are 'dana' - alms, giving, generosity, 'maitri' - love, dearness, and 'karuna' - sympathy, compassion. The 'right resolve' also contains 'sraddha', that is confidence and devotion, 'upeksa' ('upekkha') or equanimity, and 'mudita', that means sympathetic joy. Four of them - dana, maitri, karuna and upekksha, in their turn, constitute 'Brahma-vihara' (sa. maitry-apramāṇa, pi. metta-appamaññā, sa. karuṇāpramāṇa, pi. karuṇā-appamaññā, sa. muditāpramāṇa, pi. mudita-appamaññā, sa. upekṣāpramāṇa, pi. upekkhā-appamaññā), which is also called 'The Four Sublime States', and following those principles is the basic method of interrelation between Buddhistm and the world, which is something we should aspire for.

Dana is one of the most important Buddhist virtues. Since dana is based not merely on the immediate transmission of values, as it might seem, but specifically on the feelings that we feel when we are giving something to others. We can highlight a few of its forms, in order to better understand the principle on which it operates and its significance in Buddhism at all. Of course, the first thing that stands out and that is the most obvious is the giving of property. Following the principles of dana, you need to share with others all the benefits that you can share, because, among other meaning, it helps to get rid of attachment to things. It is also important that dana as well as many other aspects of the teachings of the Buddha is not an abstract rule or tradition, it is one of the fundamental principles of relations in society, which has undoubtedly changed the world for the better.

Apart from material values we can share, for example, our wisdom, which is very important for Buddhism as wisdom should not be monopolized by an individual, and shall be the heritage of all mankind to which everyone should have the right of access. We can also pass around our confidence, supporting people in difficult moment for them, which will also apply to the given. In addition, of course, we can donate to someone our time and energy even our life and health, and, of course, the most important gift of all is considered among the gift of truth - the gift of knowledge and wisdom that leading us to Enlightenment. Thus, in fact, any donation is related to dana, regardless of its importance and volume, which, as we know, are not always in correspondence with modern ideas about the donations, which in today's world are narrowed only to material goods.

Maitri (Sanskrit) or Metta (Pali) in Buddhism means benevolence, friendliness, amity, friendship, good will or kindness. In contrast, to modern Western ideas about love, which often related to the search of a sexual partner and family; maitri implies a feeling akin to love for the closest friend without sexual connotations. Ideally, love is not just for one person but cover the whole world, which is what we have to seek for, constantly developing this feeling. Thus the true Buddhist wishes all the best to every living thing, and helps with everything what he can do.

"In this case, monks, a monk cultivate the enlightenment-factor of mindfulness accompanied by loving-kindness and similarly the enlightenment-factors of investigation-of-states, energy, rapture, tranquillity, concentration, equanimity, accompanied by loving-kindness which is based on detachment, dispassion, leading to maturity of surrender. If he wishes to dwell perceiving the repulsive in what is not repulsive, he dwells thus perceiving the repulsive. If he wishes to dwell perceiving the unrepulsive in what is repulsive, he dwells thus perceiving the unrepulsive. If he wishes to dwell perceiving the repulsive both in what is repulsive and what is not repulsive, if he wishes to dwell perceiving the unrepulsive in both..., he dwells thus. If he wishes, avoiding both the repulsive and unrepulsive, to dwell equanimous, mindful and clearly aware, he dwells thus, equanimous, mindful and clearly aware, or, attaining the heart's release called 'beautiful' he abides there. I declare that the heart's release by loving-kindness has the beautiful for its excellence. This is the attainment of a wise monk who penetrates to no higher release."[1]

The next principle related to 'The Positive Aspect of Perfect Emotion' called Karuna- means compassion. According to the Buddha's teaching, compassion as an emotion is a condition very similar to love, but felt only in a relation to all living beings, who is going through some difficulties in his or her life, and because of this, love for him is magnified. This

---

[1] SN 46.54, Mettam Sutta: The Brahma-viharas, translated from the Pali by Maurice O'Connell Walshe

is the most spiritually ascended feeling among all feelings that are inherent to people. From the point of view of many practitioners of Buddhism, compassion is the most important point on the path to enlightenment, as it is thanks to the compassion the Buddha began the path to enlightenment. Some also believe that in order to achieve enlightenment is is enough to simply learn and practice karuna, because the Path of the Buddha's teaching is, in the first place, based on the practice and mutual assistance, leading to immediate use, rather than on the cultivation and multiplication of theoretical knowledge about Buddhism.

That is what the Buddha said about the goal of cultivating release by compassion: "In this, monks, a monk cultivates the enlightenment-factors of mindfulness... equanimity accompanied by compassion... he dwells thus, equanimous, mindful, clearly aware, or by passing utterly beyond all perception of objects, by the going-down of perceptions of sensory reactions, by disregarding perceptions of diversity, thinking 'space is infinite,' he attains and dwells in the sphere of infinite space. I declare that the heart's release by compassion has the sphere of infinite space for its excellence. This is the attainment of a wise monk who penetrates to no higher release."[1]

The next component of 'The Positive Aspect of Perfect Emotion' is Mudita - 'rejoice' - that is a sense of joy that arises at the sight of the joy of others, and the sharing of joy with others. This seems to be simple and intuitive principle but in practice it is not always valid, especially when confronted with the views of the Western world, where people are more often inclined to negative emotions, such as jealousy, for having learned about the success of others. Cynical attitudes, which are so popular in today's world, suggest rather

---

[1] Ibid...

gloating for failures of the others and envy for the success of the others, which is undoubtedly a selfish approach. The point is that instead of the principle of competition, where everyone wants to take first place, ahead of the others, the Buddha offers us the principle of global cooperation based on a mutual understanding, love and respect, which is much more productive from a global perspective. However, this path is to some extent the opposite of the ideal conditions of capitalism where people produce more and more new benefits only for their own satisfaction, and competing in this senseless business.

"In this, monks, a monk cultivates the enlightenment-factors of mindfulness... equanimity accompanied by sympathetic joy...he dwells thus, equanimous, mindful, clearly aware or, by passing utterly beyond the sphere of infinite space, thinking 'consciousness is infinite,' he attains and dwells in the sphere of infinite consciousness. I declare that the heart's release by sympathetic joy has the sphere of infinite consciousness for its excellence. This is the attainment of a wise monk who penetrates to no higher release."[1]

Upekksha (捨/abandon) - a term for tranquility - is a serene state of mind, which is a common human condition; however, in consequence of evolution, the mankind has started to increasingly forget about it. Above all contributed to this, as for me, the industrial revolution of the twentieth century, when more and more new discoveries have been mad has extremely accelerated the rhythm of modern life, which sometimes seems completely impossible to break out of it, and because of that, many people think that the constant anxiety and stress is characteristic for a human initially.

---

1   Ibid...

In practice, Upekksha (abandon) is resolve of unattachment to anything, letting go of greed and selfishness, and self-centered view. Calmly when people disparage, defame…is characteristic of Upekksha; unnattachment to wealth, lust, fame… is the wisdom of Upekksha; the resolve is not caught up in opposition of the duality, in a state of 'nothingness', so one is not tied by sufferings and afflictions, and can live inc states of bliss and peace.

"In this case, monks, a monk cultivates the enlightenment-factors of mindfulness, investigation-of-states, energy, rapture, tranquillity, concentration, equanimity accompanied by equanimity which is based on detachment, dispassion, leading to maturity of surrender. If he wishes to dwell... he dwells thus, equanimous, mindful and clearly aware. Or by passing utterly beyond the sphere of infinite consciousness, thinking 'there is nothing,' he attains and dwells in the sphere of nothingness. I declare that the heart's release by equanimity had the sphere of nothingness for its excellence. This is the attainment of a wise monk who penetrates to no higher release."[1]

As it was mentioned above, 'sraddha' means trust and loyalty. Do not confuse it with Western notions of faith, plaiting them here, as soon as 'sraddha' means our Right resolve to the truth and our respond to it. What is also included in the concept of 'sraddha' is respect to the three "jewels" of Buddhism which consist of Buddha, Dharma and Sangha.

In conclusion, the Right Resolve centered 3 meanings: resolve of detachment, resolve of rageless and resolve of harmless." The 'resolve of detachment' is to let go of greed and craving; 'resolve of rageless' is to eradicate hatred, and

---

[1] Ibid…

develop metta; the 'resolve of harmless' is the elimination of murder, arising. And the resolve is also divided into three categories: Wrong resolve, Right Resolve of leakage (āsava dhammā), and Right resolve of no leakage (no-āsava dhammā). The 'wrong resolve' is lust, anger, and hurt oneself and others. The 'Right resolve of leakage' is the renunciation of desires, no anger, and harmless. And the 'Right resolve of no leakage' is the resolve of achievements of sacred mind, no leakage mind; it is thinking of a saint. This resolve is result of diligent practice in Noble Path.[1]

To the term of society, the 'Right resolve of leakage' is capable to prevent the negative feelings, bad desires, and stop the arising in our anger and aversion that harm us and others. The 'Right resolve of leakage' is also thinking of human development with a perfect heart; how ideal the society is if everyone would have such thinking, and when each person has no much greed, anger and hurt each other!

---

[1]《巴利大藏經·長部》（ 卷22《大念處經》 ）："諸比庫，什麼是正思惟呢？出離思惟、無恚思惟、無害思惟。諸比庫，這稱為正思惟。 《清淨道論》第九品："以維持有情的利益行相為相。取來有情的利益為味（作用），惱害的調伏為現起（現狀），見有情的可愛為足處（近因），嗔恚的止息為（慈的）成就，產生愛著為（慈的）失敗。 《清淨道論》第九品："以拔除有情之苦的行相為相，不堪忍他人之苦為味，不害為現起 見為苦所迫者的無所依估為足處，害的止息為（悲的）成就，生憂則為（悲者）失敗." 《巴利大藏经·中部》（ 卷117 ）："欲思惟、嗔思惟、害思惟，諸比庫！此等為邪思惟。" 《巴利大藏經·中部》（ 卷117 ）："出離思惟、無嗔思惟、無害思惟，諸比庫！此等是正思惟之有漏而有福分、有持依果." 巴利大藏經·中部》（ 卷117 ）："以成就聖心、無漏心、聖道者，修習聖道結果之思擇、思惟、專注、細專注、心之專精、語行，諸比庫！此等為正思惟之聖、無漏、出世而有道支者。"

6.3 RIGHT SPEECH (samyag-vāc / sammā-vācā)

The next stage of the Eightfold Path is considered to be 'Right speech' (samyag-vāc / sammā-vācā). Right Speech is especially important in the teachings of Buddha. As we know, it is one of the significant differences between man and animal. It is believed that due to the emergence of oral language and later writing, humanity has evolved so fast, because the opportunity to share their personal experiences among the descendants and transferring useful knowledge from generation to generation. In addition, speech-this is one of those things that everyone uses on a daily basis: we use it to communicate, thus it constitutes the main part of the tools that humanity uses to communicate in whatever field it was. Without speech it would be impossible to achieve such a development of art, science and other institutions, which are the main constituent parts necessary for the development of mankind.

In most of western philosophical and religious systems, human divided into two different parts -- body and soul that symbolizes and points us to the equivalent importance, significance and value of these two main parts. On the other hand, in same oriental systems, especially in those who have a particular attitude to Buddhism, it accepted the division of man into three parts: body, speed and mind. In this partition, each of these parts corresponds to one of the three parts of human body: the heart, head and neck, respectively. Because 'speech center' is located between the other two - the head and the heart - in human's throat, it serves as a kind of bridge between them, and combining the features of both -- the first and the second one. With the speech center, we express our emotions feelings and thoughts, sharing them with others.

As it seen from above, the speech in Buddhism is paid a lot of attention, and therefore, there are some instructions that regulate this sphere of our existence. One of these rules has already been discussed above in the analysis of the five sacred precepts of Buddhism-the fourth of which teaches us to avoid deception. However, just to avoiding the lie is always not enough to reach the level of truly 'right speech'. As a start, we should determine clearly, which things are really worth to talk about, and which ones in some cases should better remain silent. The following the Buddha's instructions will help us to understand how to say much better:

1. 'In the case of words that the Tathagata knows to be unfactual, untrue, unbeneficial (or: not connected with the goal), unendearing & disagreeable to others, he does not say them.'

2. 'In the case of words that the Tathagata knows to be factual, true, unbeneficial, unendearing & disagreeable to others, he does not say them.'

3. 'In the case of words that the Tathagata knows to be factual, true, beneficial, but unendearing & disagreeable to others, he has a sense of the proper time for saying them.'

4. 'In the case of words that the Tathagata knows to be unfactual, untrue, unbeneficial, but endearing & agreeable to others, he does not say them.'

5. 'In the case of words that the Tathagata knows to be factual, true, unbeneficial, but endearing & agreeable to others, he does not say them.'

6. 'In the case of words that the Tathagata knows to be factual, true, beneficial, and endearing & agreeable to others, he has a sense of the proper time for saying them. Why is that? Because the Tathagata has sympathy for living beings."[1]

---

[1] MN 58, Abhaya Sutta: To Prince Abhaya

(Tathāgata - one of the Buddhas names, which translation means 'one who has thus gone' (tathā-gata) or 'one who has thus come' (tathā-āgata):

It is noticeable that the set of rules above is seems to be more suited for the self-controlling rather than for self-development, but this is only a small part of what is meant by 'right speech'. The concept is much broader; it covers a lot of important areas of human being, helping us to streamline the relationship between people in general. The Buddha describes right speech as follows: "And what is right speech? Abstaining from lying, from divisive speech, from abusive speech, and from idle chatter: This is called right speech. It is spoken at the right time. It is spoken in truth. It is spoken affectionately. It is spoken beneficially. It is spoken with a mind of good-will."[1]

Thus, on the assumption of the Buddha's words, we can highlight the following essential elements of the right of speech: it must be completely truthful, has to express affectionateness, and has to be helpful and useful for the interlocutor, as well as it has to promote harmony and eliminating disagreements between people. Each of those things is a standard measure of correct speech; they knowingly placed in such order to show us different stages of communication between people, which one of them follows from the previous one, complementing and deepening its meaning.

The first criterion, of course, is the truthfulness of speech. The truth in this context means not only an accurate statement of the facts, but also the lack of unsaid things, which could be important, and complete sincerity. Thus, unsetting forth the facts and attempts to hide anything, will

---

[1] SN 45.8, Magga-vibhanga Sutta: An Analysis of the Path

lead to deviation from right speech principles. It seems to be uneasy task to match those criteria, but it is quite possible to do; however, to perform this step for each person should be honest with oneself.

We have to understand clearly what we think and what we feel, especially, because in the modern world, this thing is constantly coming from outside information and constantly puts pressure on us with creating chaos and confusion. Each of us has a lot of ideas and thoughts, but many thoughts in our minds; if we analyze are not our own, but imposed on us by various authorities, and sometimes to get to the real root is not so simple. On the other hand, we have feelings that are totally individual and come from within, but often we can not understand and entangled in their own emotions, because often do not even know how to cope with them. Most of the principles guiding our behavior in different situations and have an impact on decision-making, imposed on us by education and ambient pressure, thus are not always right or even necessary. Honesty requires constant awareness and analysis of their actions, thoughts and feelings. Based on this, it is enough difficult to meet the truth and to be really honest, as required by Buddhism.

In order to achieve the veracity of our speech, we need only to follow along, then to reach the next stage of "right speech" we have to think of others before saying. The friendliness of our speech, in the modern sense, again, moved away far enough from the initial value, and in particular on the values attributed to this criterion Buddhism. Friendliness is not just a set of polite cliche or kind words, which it is accepted to use if you want to express to anyone with respect or just seem polite. Often, talking to people we perceive them through the prism of their own beliefs, and evaluate them only based on our own experience; respectively, the feelings that we feel for the people depend only on our own preferences and desires rather reflecting our inner world. True friendliness is a manifestation of love for the other person, but guided by generally accepted views; our love the most is from our attitude to the behavior of people than the people themselves. The manifestation of true friendliness implies the awareness of the other person as same as yourself objectively and separate from yourself.

Only after realization and acceptance of the demands and needs of other people as our own, we will be able to interact with them, going to the third stage of the Right Speech, which is helpfulness. Speaking about the helpfulness of speech, we are talking primarily about how what we say will help a person to get back on the right path, and to ascend to a higher level of awareness and to being closer to enlightenment. In this context, the ability to properly convey certain information is very important. We must learn to see the good side in everything because for interlocutor the mood he gets while talking with someone is always important, and this will always effect to cheer a person. On the other hand, in the modern world, aggressive criticism is used far more often, and criticism that confuses and breaks the connection between human beings and; as practice shows, this path leads to the opposite side by the harmony among people.

So we got to the last stage of Right Speech - the need for harmony and understanding among people. In fact, this aspect of speech combines the three previous ones, because if we go through them, if we understand, recognize and love other people, we will understand the needs and demands of other people to help each other to grow spiritually that based on truthfulness, awareness and love. How can such state of collective consciousness not lead to a complete harmony and understanding?

Higher aspect, The Buddha advised practitioners to stay away funny words, useless words, and just focus on the ten destinations following in conversation: desireless, contentment, renunciation, away from the bondages, diligence, discipline, concentration, wisdom, liberation, and liberation out of knowledge.[1] To achieve fully liberation, might be everyone should be based on ten criterias above to know what point of his (her) right speech is reached.

6.4 RIGHT ACTION (samyak-karmānta / sammā-kammanta)

The fourth stage of the Eightfold Path is called Right Action (samyak-karmanta; Pali: samma-kammanta), and specifies the form and procedure to be followed on the path to enlightenment. Most lay people are accustomed to the fact that this formulation implies a basic relation to morals and ethics, a certain universal set of rules, according to which every act and is defined as true or false. Something like this set of rules we can call the Five Precepts; however, it is not the only commandment, and the main criterion, as it can not handle all the action. Five commandments only show us the things that do not cost, for one reason or another, being the first criterion.

However, apart from the above, in Buddhism the ideal 'not-doing' is also very important action, and the central criterion for its justification and necessity is awareness. You must be fully committed to Right Action and be aware of what is happening, constantly thinking about the consequences of your actions. It is important to the concept of causality because our every action has its consequences, from which much depends. To sum up, each committed action brings us pain or pleasure, depending on it, and should make the

---

[1] 巴利大藏经·增支部 (卷10章69)

decision. Therefore, it turns out that we are up against the question of intelligence because the understanding of causality and competent use is possible only with its help. Whereby, actions in Buddhism are divided into skillful and unskillful to be explained in responding to our problems that the Buddha divides them as follows:

"Now what is unskillful? Taking life is unskillful, taking what is not given ... sexual misconduct ... lying ... abusive speech ... divisive tale-bearing ... idle chatter is unskillful. Covetousness ... ill will ... wrong views are unskillful. These things are termed unskillful. And what are the roots of what is unskillful? Greed is a root of what is unskillful; aversion is a root of what is unskillful; delusion is a root of what is unskillful. These are termed the roots of what is unskillful."

"And what is skillful? Abstaining from taking life is skillful, abstaining from taking what is not given ... from sexual misconduct ... from lying ... from abusive speech ... from divisive tale-bearing ... abstaining from idle chatter is skillful. Lack of covetousness ... lack of ill will ... right views are skillful. These things are termed skillful. And what are the roots of what is skillful? Lack of greed is a root of what is skillful; lack of aversion is a root of what is skillful; lack of delusion is a root of what is skillful. These are termed the roots of what is skillful."[1]

According to Buddhism, the proper action should be as nourishment for humans, respectively, every action must contribute to the growth and promotion to get rid of suffering and attain enlightenment, and to provide energy for future efficiencies and maintain life better.

"There are these four nutriments for the maintenance of

---

[1] MN 9, Sammaditthi Sutta: translated from the Pali by Ñanamoli Thera & Bhikkhu Bodhi

beings that have come into being or for the support of those in search of a place to be born. Which four? Physical food, gross or refined, contacts as the second, intellectual intention the third, and consciousness the fourth; from the origination of craving comes the origination of nutriment. From the cessation of craving comes the cessation of nutriment."[1]

Being one of the fundamental consequences of the actions of each person, fourth nutriment principle should be used very skillfully. When they are assumed as nutrition, life-sustaining and developing by them, and the lack of them, so anything can be eradicated. Therefore, the consequences of these actions can be very different, for the demands of the body and thoughts-the matter is how we nourish our body and mind in skilful or unskillful thing; we should definitely contemplate when thoughts arise, starting to some matter, asking thinking that is negative or positive by ourselves.

Just do not forget about what emotions we invest in their actions, as Right Action - the fourth of the steps of the Eightfold Path, expressed by the action from the Right View and Perfect Emotion, and helping us on the path to enlightenment. Also, we should know that Right Action ideally requires a full dedication, when the execution of an action directed all the essence and energy of man, all his physical strength, all his wisdom, and all compassion and all the love. Of course, it is quite difficult to put all their energies to fulfill the purpose, not being distracted by external factors, but concentrating fully on it their whole essence. Accordingly, the concentration ability is of great value in this context, and, of course, requires constant training.

Thus, Right Action implies quite rigorous analysis of your own actions, involving a careful thought in this,

---

[1] Ibid...

instead of just following a set of rules. While starting the implementation of an action, if you are following the word of the Buddha, you should first make sure there is not contrary to the commandments of the five action plans, and then to think about the potential consequences both positive and negative to avoid the latter. Keep in mind that every action eventually brings pain or joy, and constantly train your mind in proper planning. In addition, you always maintain mindfulness and focus on certain emotion in any circumstance, as Right Action it is also an integral action to which all the physical and mental force is directed. From this it follows that Right Action implies and regulates not only the fact of the correctness of the action with respect to the Buddha's teachings, but also the constant training of the mind in order to achieve the maximum effect of their actions. In Buddhism, there are also practices that help to develop our minds to more exalted states of consciousness and existence in general. It is believed that the best method for such developing is meditation, which is practiced in the context of the Buddhist spiritual life called 'bhavana'. According to the Buddha's teaching, there are four higher states of mind; each of them is more advanced, than the previous one. Thus, success in mind development is measured as an attainment of a higher level of the Right action, which is called dhyanas (Sanskrit, Pali - jhanas). It seems to be impossible to describe them, as they completely change the structure of the inner and outer world. In such case, the Buddha gave their description in a figurative, metaphorical way; to which in essence, there is nothing to add.

The first dhyana is a first one of the higher meditative states. To enter the first dhyana, as the Buddha says, the only way to reach it is to become withdrawn from sensuality, withdrawn from wrong ations, and withdrawn from unskillful qualities; after reaching it, people become filled with joy and delight which have arisen due to successful searches of wisdom. 'There is nothing of his entire body unpervaded by rapture and pleasure born from withdrawa; this one state of mind could be compared to soap mixed with water: 'Just as if a skilled bathman or bathman's apprentice would pour bath powder into a brass basin and knead it together, sprinkling it again and again with water, so that his ball of bath powder - saturated, moisture-laden, permeated within and without - would nevertheless not drip; even so, the monk permeates, suffuses and fills this very body with the rapture and pleasure born of withdrawal. There is nothing of his entire body unpervaded by rapture and pleasure born from withdrawal...'[1]

To reach the second level, a monk has to attain a state of calm down from rapture and pleasure due to his directed Right action of thoughts and evaluations. To show us the essence of the second dhyana, the Buddha told "Just like a lake with spring-water welling up from within, having no inflow from east, west, north, or south, and with the skies periodically supplying abundant showers, so that the cool fount of water welling up from within the lake would permeate and pervade, suffuse and fill it with cool waters, there being no part of the lake unpervaded by the cool waters; even so, the monk permeates and pervades, suffuses and fills this very body with the rapture and pleasure born of composure. There is nothing of his entire body unpervaded by rapture and pleasure born of composure..."[2]

After passing a second level of mind, monk has a chance to go even further with the fading of rapture state, he remains

---

[1] AN 5.28, Samadhanga Sutta: The Factors of Concentration

[2] Ibid...

equanimous, mindful, and alert, and senses pleasure along with his body. The simile for the third dhyana state is: 'Just as in a blue-, white-, or red-lotus pond, there may be some of the blue, white, or red lotuses which born and growing in the water, stay immersed in the water and flourish without standing up out of the water, so that they are permeated and pervaded, suffused and filled with cool water from their roots to their tips, and nothing of those blue, white, or red lotuses would be unpervaded with cool water; even so, the monk permeates and pervades, suffuses and fills this very body with the pleasure divested of rapture. There is nothing of his entire body unpervaded with pleasure divested of rapture...'[1]

The final, the highest of meditative states or dhyanas is only available for those who had overcome the states of pleasure and the stress and the difference between them, as rising above the distinction of them. According to the Buddha's words, its definition is following: "And furthermore, with the abandoning of pleasure and stress - as with the earlier disappearance of elation and distress - he enters and remains in the fourth jhana: purity of equanimity and mindfulness, neither-pleasure-nor-pain. He sits, permeating the body with a pure, bright awareness, so that there is nothing of his entire body unpervaded by pure, bright awareness."[2]

Thefore, the Right Action is conducts correcting that based on two aspects: body and mind. In term of body, Buddha advised laypeople to practice five precepts[3] and avoid all the other evils, for making the happiness, and peace for oneself and others. Further, for those who are on the path to enlightenment, the Buddha has suggested the

---

[1] Ibid...

[2] Ibid...

[3] 《巴利大藏经·长部》（ 卷22《大念处经》 ）：諸比庫，什麼是正業呢？離殺生、離不與取、離欲邪行。諸比庫，這稱為正業.

four meditative states to keep the mind detach from desires, pleasures, thoughts and attachments which cause stress and pain for inner and obscure the pure light of ours mind. Practicing Right Action, the body's always in good conducts, the thingking's always mindfulness, and equanimity; there is also the whole meaning of the Buddha's teachings.

> *"Every evil never doing*
> *And in wholesomeness increasing*
> *And one's heart well-purifying:*
> *This is the Buddha's Teaching."*[1]

(Sabbapapassa akaranaj
Kusalassa upasampada
Sacittapariyodapanaj
Etaj buddhana sasanaj)

6.5 *RIGHT LIVELIHOOD* (samyag-vyāyāma / sammā-vāyāma)

The next stage of Eightfold Path is called Right Livelihood (samyag-ājīva / sammā-ājīva). It is a vocation to feed you and your family and their families on the principles of the Buddha, and earning benefits in the way of no harm to other beings. In Buddhism, Right Livelihood includes self-interest and for others; in addition to support yourself, the compassion also must be nourished; lack of compassion, your livelihood becomes wrong livelihood which causing bad karma you could not be unamenable.

Sangharakshita discusses it in a relation to the concept of an ideal society - which, in his opinion, is one of the main purposes of Buddhism. In this connection, Sangharakshita firstly says that we all, even the greatest of us, dream of a perfect world, which is inhabited by a perfect society, and

---

[1] DhP3/Translated by Ven. Weragoda Sarada Maha Thero

this utopia dreaming is just a way to rise above our routine existence. Such dreams may be a vision of New Jerusalem in Bible, Republic of Plato, Campanella's City of the Sun, Utopia of Thomas More, etc, and Buddhism also suggests us a concept of a pure land - Sukhāvatī, the 'Western paradise', in which there is no suffering, no pain, no diseases, no conflicts, even misunderstandings, and so on: there is even no bad weather in Sukhāvatī. However, Sangharakshita stresses out that Buddhism is not about mere dreams; on the contrary, it is very practical - because it aims at creating a new perfect society here, on our planet, and in our countries and homes. So Sangharakshita argues that the fifth stage of Eightfold Path represents a transformation of our society into new one.[1]

Further, in his writing, Sangharashita assumes that all previous stages concern the changes of individual experience, experiences of separated beings while this stage already concerns a society, as a collective experience. Because of that, he wonders why among all spheres of collective existence (according to Sangharashita, there are three: strictly social sphere, political sphere, and economical sphere), on the fifth stage of his noble guidance, the Buddha limited himself with only economical aspect, and why he only taught about moneymaking? Sangharashita makes an attempt to answer by himself: it is plainly because of a social situation in India: most people were not into politics, and the caste system mostly determined all the social interrelations, so the only thing that concerned all the Indians was what they did for living-their labor. That is why obviously the Buddha considered the economical aspect of collective existence to be the most essential and made it a part of the Eightfold Path.[2]

---

[1] Sangharakshita, The Buddha's Noble Eightfold Path, p.58-59

[2] Ibid..., p.61-62

Finally, Sangharashita proceeds to analyze the concept of Perfect Livelihood. It is obvious from Buddhist worldview that when we dedicate a lot of time and effort to our work, it has a serious impact on our mind and body, and the majority of people in the world work, and jobs a lot. The author suggests an example of a man who works in a slaughterhouse, and wonders how terribly his psychic transforms after instant killings of living beings. He also provides a statistics that 66% of slaughterhouse workers have serious mental issues.[1] And the slaughterhouse is only a grain in the sand: there are millions of jobs that cause irreversible damage to our nature, obscure our minds, and escalate our suffering. That is why the concept of Right Livelihood is so important, and more and more Buddhists in the world quit their former jobs for that reason.

The stage of Right Livelihood implies that it is wrong (or wrong livelihood) to make for living under such conditions which eventually will destroy you on the path to Enlightenment. The Buddha said: "And what, monks, is right livelihood? There is the case where a disciple of the noble ones, having abandoned dishonest livelihood and keeps his life going with right livelihood: This, monks, is called right livelihood.[2] One should ensure that his way of living is righteous: legal, peaceful, honest, and has no harming consequences to yourself and other living beings.

The Buddha emphasized five kinds of activities that are most harmful to engage in:

1) Activities, related to making and selling gun, as well as other weapons of destruction.

2) Activities, related to trading other living beings, such as slave trade or prostitution.

---

[1] Ibid..., p.63

[2] SN 45.8, Magga-vibhanga Sutta: An Analysis of the Path

3) Activities, related to production of meat, because it needs killing a living being.

4) Activities, related to intoxicants, which influence the state of our consciousness, such as drugs and alcohol.

5) Activities, related to making or selling poisons, which are designed to kill; in times of Gautama Buddha there even existed such a profession: a person you can come to and buy poison for a murder.[1]

Sangharashita comments that even a slight relation to those activities inevitably brings bad karma. For example, you may have only one per cent of shares in a company that produces or keeps nuclear weapon not being involved in it physically, and by that you are still responsible for that; you are the one that helps to produce nuclear weapon, so from Buddhist point of view, you are on the wrong path.[2]

Other bad occupations mentioned by the Buddha are those that deal with trickery (e.g. conjurors), deceit (e.g. lots of news reporters nowadays, politicians…), usury (e.g. pawnshop keepers), and soothsaying (fortune tellers, astrologists).[3] Even actors were disapproved by the Buddha, who answering to one actor's questions, said that actors not only fail to go to heaven, but actually, go to hell because they most of all contribute to degradation of other people, and sharing their vanity to the audiences.[4] However, basically, any job that violates the principles of right action and right speech, or has harmful consequences to anybody are considered wrong livelihood by Buddhists.

After following through the concept of Right Livelihood,

---

[1] AN5:177, Vanijja Sutta, Business (Wrong Livelihood)

[2] Sangharakshita, The Buddha's Noble Eightfold Path, p.65

[3] MN 117, Maha-cattarisaka Sutta: The Great Forty

[4] Sangharakshita, The Buddha's Noble Eightfold Path, p.65-66

we should try to apply it to the modern world, because society has gone through major economic changes since fifth century B.C. Sangharashita helps us with that by dividing this concept into three subsections: occupation, vocation, and duration.[1]

Occupations, in their turn, can be divided into four categories: First type of occupations is harmful ones, which we discussed above - they cannot be righteous in any case. Second category is not negative occupation, but it also influences people in a bad way, cultivates destructive emotions, in them, such as greed, those are occupations of advertisers, and spammers on the Internet and so on. Third category is those occupations that can be transformed into a rightful path if we make some efforts, for example, something usual as working in the office as a manager. The last category is those occupations, which do not require a lot of mental pressure, those are the simplest jobs; and Sangharashita recommends the good aspects for Buddhists so that nothing took their energy from the level which is sufficient to meditate.[2]

For the vocation, Sangharashita defines it as "a means of livelihood which is directly related to what one considers of ultimate importance in one's life."[3] It is just vocation when someone considers his or her job to be a pleasure-not labor. This is rare and individual, but it is actually that perfect state we are seeking for with the help of Buddhism.

Duration section is about how much time a certain work takes from worker and is it worth it. Often greed for money and things (like Apple products which became desire and

---

[1] Ibid...

[2] Ibid...

[3] Ibid...

obsession in our time) obscures our minds, and we devote ourselves to constant money-making process, which brings us only stress and material goods that are imposed on us from TV screens, Internet and lots of our colleagues and friends who fell on the wave of yielding 'success'. When working, especially that one which does not really add anything good into this world, is taking all the energy of the individual he cannot become a Buddhist, because the path of the Bodhisattva requires a lot of dedication.

Our global economy complicates the precautions to do no harm to others. For example, you have a job in a processing workshop that related to damaging to the environment, working in food processing company from animals, working in a company of producing beer and wine, working in a branch of being exploiting the labor of others, or working for a coporation of product competing ... For to feed ourself and our family, we are no longer a choice, so we have to continue. However, do not forget that we are still responsible for what we did. If we remember that all beings are interconnected, we can find another way to separate ourself from anything 'impure' is impossible and bad karma really; thus, we do not hurt our love and compassion. Master Thich Nhat Hanh wrote: "To practice Right Livelihood (samyag ajiva), you have to find a way to earn your living without transgressing your ideals of love and compassion. The way you support yourself can be an expression of your deepest self, or it can be a source of suffering for you and others. " ... Our vocation can nourish our understanding and compassion, or erode them. We should be awake to the consequences, far and near, of the way we earn our living."[1]

Thus, for every lay Buddhist, refusing to wrong livelihood, to what damage for all livings, and following to the motto of

---

[1] The Heart of the Buddha's Teaching, Parallax Press, 1998, p. 104

the love and compassion, so the one is called to live in Right Livelihood. Earning to nourish yourself and your family but is not cause suffering for other beings, that is conscious life, and your life is meaningful for youself and others. Highly developed, The Buddha also encourage the monks keeping to beg for food as Shangha virture, and he also emphasizes to nourish the mind with abandon all desires, mindfulness, practicing noble path to attain transcendent mind, as Mahācattārīsaka Sutta in Majjhima Nikaya following:

"And what is right livelihood? Right Livelihood, I tell you, is of two sorts: There is right livelihood with effluents, siding with merit, resulting in acquisitions; there is right livelihood that is noble, without effluents, transcendent, a factor of the path.

"And what is the right livelihood with effluents, siding with merit, resulting in acquisitions? There is the case where a disciple of the noble ones abandons wrong livelihood and maintains his life with right livelihood. This is the right livelihood with effluents, siding with merit, resulting in acquisitions.

"And what is the right livelihood that is noble, without effluents, transcendent, a factor of the path? The abstaining, desisting, abstinence, avoidance of wrong livelihood in one developing the noble path whose mind is noble, whose mind is without effluents, who is fully possessed of the noble path."[1]

---

[1] MN 117, Maha-cattarisaka Sutta: The Great Forty

6.6 RIGHT EFFORT (samyak-vyāyāma / sammā-vāyāma)

Right Effort (samyak-vyāyāma / sammā-vāyāma) is the sixth principle of the Noble Eightfold Path. Vyayama means effort, and Samyak means perfect, so it is Perfect Effort, and sometimes it is translated as 'right effort'. Another definition of it is Right convenience- means the proper effort to avoid bad and do good things; self-enlightenment effort; making unborn evil cannot be born, and the evil was born then stopped; making unborn kindness can be born, and the kindness was born then can achieved perfection.

This factor also implies that a practitioner applies a sustained effort to throw away all detrimental and harmful thoughts to words and deeds. At the same time, efforts are made to develop positive and good thoughts, words and actions with respecting both to ourself and to others, and all that under condition that would not cause difficulties and tediousness for the efforts to eliminate the evil and develop the good things. The Buddha himself gives a definition for a Right Effort principle:

"And what, monks, is right effort?

[i] "There is the case where a monk generates desire, endeavors, activates persistence, upholds & exerts his intent for the sake of the non-arising of evil, unskillful qualities that have not yet arisen.

[ii] He generates desire, endeavors, activates persistence, upholds & exerts his intent for the sake of the abandonment of evil, unskillful qualities that have arisen.

[iii] He generates desire, endeavors, activates persistence, upholds & exerts his intent for the sake of the arising of skillful qualities that have not yet arisen.

[iv] He generates desire, endeavors, activates persistence, upholds & exerts his intent for the maintenance, non-confusion, increase, plenitude, development, & culmination of skillful qualities that have arisen: This, monks, is called right effort."[1]

Sangharashita recalls that second, third and fourth parts of the Eightfold Path were related to the personal transformation of individual, and the fifth one concerned a society as a whole. With the sixth stage of Perfect Effort, we return to the topic of individual transformation, especially, to the transformation of the individual will, but influential platform of the Right effort is to have a lot of social inclusion by its impacts. This background is actually the whole world of living beings and the whole process of evolution. For that reason, the Perfect Effort, in fact, symbolizes that spiritual life is considered to be a culmination of the whole evolutionary process-the conscious evolution of Man.[2]

It is also symbolical that in many languages of modern India (Hindi, the Marathi, and Gujerati) the word vyāyāma is used to denote physical exercises, especially associated with gymnastics. In the context of the Noble Eightfold Path and Buddhism at all, this fact focuses our attention on the activity and dynamism of the spiritual life. Buddhists are not those who read sutras about the efforts of other people while sitting with a cup of tea on an armchair by the fireplace even if they do it every day. In spiritual life, we actually have to make efforts, not necessarily physical efforts, but mostly mental efforts, because a path to Nirvana is a hard path, as it is extremely difficult to clear our body and mind from the poisons.[3]

---

[1] SN 45.8, Magga-vibhanga Sutta: An Analysis of the Path

[2] Sangharashita, p. 70

[3] Ibid, p.70-71

Sangharashita emphasizes that there are two sorts of effort in Buddhist worldview. There is a perfect effort in general, and there is a special perfect effort which is a sixth stage of the Noble Eightfold Path. Nevertheless, some kind of effort is needed at the every stage of the Path. This aspect we can illustrate with the words of the Buddha:

"One tries to abandon wrong view & to enter into right view: This is one's right effort...

"One tries to abandon wrong resolve & to enter into right resolve: This is one's right effort...

"One tries to abandon wrong speech & to enter into right speech: This is one's right effort...

"One tries to abandon wrong action & to enter into right action: This is one's right effort...

"One tries to abandon wrong livelihood & to enter into right livelihood: This is one's right effort."[1]

Perfect Effort as a sixth stage of the Noble Eightfold Path consists of exercises that are recommended for a practice to train the perfect effort with the Four Exertions: preventing, eradicating, developing, and maintaining. Those actions hold as an object that so-called skillful and unskillful mental states. Unskillful mental state is "one that is contaminated by craving or selfish desire, by hatred, or by delusion, mental confusion, bewilderment, and lack of perspective."[2] Therefore, preventing is recognizing that one of those states is going to come and preventing ourself from the unskillful situation when these feelings possess our consciousness - simply letting it to pass by our mind.

Eradicating is clearing our thoughts from those unskillful

---

[1] MN 17, Vanapatthasutta

[2] Sangharashita, p. 73

mental states when they have already occurred. There is a Buddhist teaching called Five Hindrances (pancanivarana) which tells us about the obstacles that usually intervenes the process of eradicating. Hindrances are the five qualities of the mind that dazzle mental vision, and make our mind weak. Because of these five hindrances practitioner cannot achieve deep meditative concentration, and therefore he is not able to clearly see the truth-the reality. These hindrances include sensory desire (kāmacchanda), hatred or ill-will (vyāpāda), restlessness and anxiety (uddhacca-kukkucca), sloth and torpor (thīna-middha), and doubt (vicikicchā).[1]

In the Suttas there is a beautiful example of the water in the tank: sensual desire is compared to water which is mixed different colors. Hated can be compared with boiling water. Laziness and lethargy as water covered with slime and algae. Restlessness and regret as water on which there is a ripple in the wind. Skeptical doubt is as the muddy water. In all of these cases, in such water it is hard to see our own reflection, just as in the case of the five mental hindrances which do not allow us to identify clearly the reality and obscure understanding of your own good, and the good of both others.

These hindrances are very deep and it is extremely difficult to completely overcome them - it requires long and full practice of the Buddhist path to do so. Practitioner is able to completely overcome the five hindrances and enter into a state of jhana in which these five hindrances are completely (or almost completely) absent. However, they are not eradicated by jhana; they can be eradicated only through the practice of insight based on jhana. The practice of insight leads to the complete eradication of these obstacles, as well as other impurities of the mind.[2]

---

[1] Ibid, p.73-74

[2] Ibid, p73-75

Unless we reached the full concentration of the mind, we can say with certainty that there is at least one obstacle, and even more. The most important thing is recognize the hindrance in the hindrance: because only by defining it as such, it is possible to oppose it.

Very often the act of recognition weakens the hindrance because it immediately reminds us that the purpose of meditation is concentration of the mind. Nevertheless, we may have a tendency to avoid this recognition. Most people have a special hindrances-characteristic only for them a way to 'protect' themselves, for example, laziness and apathy can successfully hide, not being able to recognize itself. This happens in the morning we do not want to get up early: first, the mind refuses to accept that the time has come to rise, and then looks for an excuse so we could lie in bed for another five minutes. When we are under the influence of will-ill, we most likely will tirelessly seek out for the faults of others, and again turn over in memory all painful and unpleasant that happened to us. It is necessary to clearly realize that we are dealing with an obstacle to concentrate the mind. There are many techniques and tricks that allow you to re-engage in the process of meditation. Those four basic antidotes are following:

The first of them is to reflect on the consequences that may result from the uncontrolled growth of hindrances. What happens if we do not work with our inclinations which make us distracted, hateful and doubtful? It is clear that they will grow if our character increasingly falls under their influence. If you think about the importance of what you do, it will once again become clear and the mind will be more inclined to concentrate.

The second way is to develop the quality of what is opposite to a certain hindrance. If there is a doubt, strengthen confidence; if there is laziness, strengthen energy; if there is concern, deepen the state of peace and tranquility; if the mind is too tense, relax it; if it wanders too much, strengthen concentration. In other words, once the path of right concentration arises how the negative state of mind arises; we aim to counterbalance it and develop a positive quality that weakens or neutralizes the obstacles encountered.

The third antidote is to engender a state of mind similar to the sky. Sometimes, the more you resist a particular state of mind, the stronger it becomes. If the above two methods do not help, try to create a mood: 'the mind is like a clear blue sky, and the hindrances are the clouds.' Working this way, we recognize that there was a hindrance, and just observe it. We are now watching how it unfolds in the space of our mind in the form of fantasies, anxieties, and images… keep track of all that occurs. We watch closely, but try not too involved in the process; otherwise, it will only 'feed' the obstacles. If we observe patiently, not too engaging, so obstacle eventually lose strength and dissipate.

The fourth antidote is suppression. It is a sort of a last resort: we just need to tell the obstacle 'no' and push him away. Suppression method is most useful when an obstacle is weak and when we firmly believe that we should not give him hospitality. If the obstacle is very large or if we are in a state of mental conflict, the use of this method may cause adverse side effects. When we are too zealous, it often causes tension, insensitivity, and carelessness of mind. Therefore, the best practical method is to use suppression only if the hindrances are weak. When the mind is clear and the attitude is positive, eradicating such a hindrance is quite easy.

Finally, if those methods cannot help, there is still so-called Refuge to the Buddha that sometimes it is impossible for us to cope with hindrances. During the entire period of practice or the greater part of the mind is completely distracted from the object of meditation, when this happens, it is very important not to despair. It is necessary to consider the practice from the point of view of the entire development process. We all have inherent strengths unconscious desires and inclinations, and the fight sometimes inevitable. We must remind ourselves that we have done everything possible, and we sincerely tried. These efforts necessarily give good results even if in this meditation we have did not have any special changes. Coming to Refuge is not much a way of dealing with hindrances, but rather a special state to communication with which we try to preserve and after a period of meditation. We need to reaffirm their commitment to practice, or in the language of tradition: come to the refuge. So, we reaffirm our commitment to the development of superior human qualities until we reach the Enlightenment (symbolized by the Buddha), his teachings (Dharma), and all those who practice it (Sangha).[1]

In summary, there are two kinds Right Effort: body effort and mind effort. The body effort is body doing good behavior, bearing all patiences to overcome the external challenges, and to achieve one's aspirations. The mind effort is to endure the unwanted things, develop positive thinkings, and eradicate evil things/mental afflictions while practice Dharma to attain perfect enlightenment and peace.[2]

---

[1] Ibid, p.74-77

[2] (《瑜伽师地论》（八十九卷）：”此中最初、当知发起猛利乐欲。次随所欲，发起坚固勇悍方便。次为证得所受诸法，不自轻蔑，亦无怯惧。次能堪忍寒热等苦。后于下劣，不生喜足；欣求后后转胜转妙诸功德住。”）
《瑜伽师地论》（八十九卷）：”此中最初、当知发起猛利乐欲。次随所欲，发起坚固勇悍方便。次为证得所受诸法，不自轻蔑，亦无怯惧。次能堪忍寒热等苦。后于下劣，不生喜足；欣求后后转胜转妙诸功德住。"

The Buddhists follow Right Effort can be gained happiness, and potentially helped others achieving some benefits actually in this life.

6.7 RIGHT MINDFULNESS (samyak-smṛti / sammā-sati)

The Mindfulness includes four foundation of mindfulness (Pāli: satipaṭṭhāna, Sanskrit: smrtyupasthana); that means to focus on body, feelings, mind and objects; four places to cultivated by mindfulness to get rid of delusion, distinguish from thingkings (awareness of impure body, awareness of distressed feelings, awareness of impermanent mind, and awareness of selfless objects). Basing on Right view, and depending on the stages of the practice through four foundation of mindfulness, we gain wisdom in differences; Buddha said: "Monks, there is a path to practice that make living beings to be pure, overcoming sadness and woefulness, removing pain and anxiety, reaching the truth, and entering in Nirvana; which are the four foundations of mindfulness."[1]

As the previous stage of eightfold pass, 'right mindfulness' (samyak-smṛti/sammā-sati), which also called 'perfect awareness', applies to meditation (Sanskrit and Pāli: samādhi) division-the presence of consciousness in all circumstances. In such case, it assumes high level of self-control over thoughts and body.

Unlike the usally thought, people think they are aware of themselves and their actions as the fullest extent; however, this is often not the case. For example, Sigmund Freud, the founder of psychoanalysis, in his book "Introduction to Psychoanalysis", he pays special attention to the little

---

[1] 巴利大藏经·长部》（卷22《大念处经》）：" 諸比庫，此一行道，能清淨有情，超越愁 、悲，滅除苦 、憂，得達如理，現證涅盤，此即是四念處 。

mistakes that are taking place in our everyday life due to various small errors that occur with us every day. More precisely, he is looking for the reasons, which cause mistakes we used to make every day: for example, in our speech by oral or written, sometimes we make mistakes when we cannot clearly make out somebody's words or incorrectly reading written words perceiving wrong information, or sometimes even inadvertently replacing some words by the other ones, cases of short-term temporary forgetting of names or concepts, or temporary loss of any items, and so on.

According to Freud, all those accidents are happening not by chance, but what they really are is a consequence of actions of our subconscious basing on our ego-which is feed upon our fears and passions. The subconscious may well deliberately displace any information from our minds or distort it according to its 'own' interests. Therefore, our desires often guide our way of thinking and feeling, and not vice versa, as is commonly believed. Right mindfulness teaches us how to purify our minds from unnecessary voices and forms, and helping us to determine which of the ideas come from what motives and to get rid of unnecessary ones.

As long as 'right mindfulness' is a step of the seventh level, it could be truly reached only with sequential process all previous stages which it is already quite a challenge; more precisely, as it had serious preparation before, this part in other sense, is a consequence of the implementation of the previous ones.

In Buddha's words, 'right mindfulness' is:

'There is the case where a monk remains focused on the body in & of itself - ardent, alert, & mindful - putting aside greed & distress with reference to the world. He remains focused on feelings in & of themselves... the mind in & of itself... mental qualities in & of themselves - ardent, alert, & mindful - putting aside greed & distress with reference to the world. This is called right mindfulness...'[1]

Thus, we see that in order to achieve this state, it is required to achieve great success in the performance of the previous stages. The emphasis is not on the fact of what the person has refused, or from how much negative biases person has cleansed, as it accepted for example in Christianity, but on what person has achieved through this; once again reminds us that the Buddha only showed us the direction which we should follow, so everyone should pass this way by himself. As the mindfulness encompasses many spheres of life, it can be divided into several sections, depending on whether specific sphere it influences, and vice versa.

In such case, for example Sangharakshita defines the following four levels of awareness, using differentiation principle, depending on the object of attention, for our better understanding of the whole concept: 'awareness of things', 'awareness of self', 'awareness other people' and 'awareness of Reality'.[2]

'Awareness of things'

In today's world, we have forgotten how to pay attention to many wonderful things, paying to them surely not enough attention, misunderstanding them, and often forgetting about their essence. The forgetfulness always happens, in the modern world, people have no time and no wish for concentrating on them.

Considering any item, often we do not perceive it in its pure form as required by the Buddha's teaching. Nowadays, awareness became particularly noticeable due to an all-out

[1] DN 22, Maha-satipatthana Sutta: The Great Frames of Reference

[2] Sangharakshita, P. 87

industrialization with its crazy rhythm of life, from which we seem so hard to escape. Living in such a rhythm, people often think that the Right mindfulness is seemingly impossible and totally 'irrational' to waste time on it. The philosophy of the modern world encourages us to consume the goods (as much as we could, or even more) without thinking about their essence, leaving no time for it, imposes on us the superficial desires, and hiding the Truth.

For example, the majority of car owners in the world do not know how to drive their car at all. Only a serious failure could get them to find it out. Most online sites or computer software users are further away from the desire to analyze anything, because even in case of serious failure the solution of these problems does not require their direct participation. It is worth remembering that above-mentioned things were created by humanity and requires more logical interpretation than 'understanding' in the Buddhist sense, the achievement of which is much more complex and difficult, but as people say 'longest way round is the shortest way home'.[1]

Awareness of things derived inside seeing: when we look at the workings of all things and situations in the presence of right mindfulness, we have accurate and deeper understanding any things; they cannot drag us along their spiral. The presence of Mindfulness is 'seeing phenomena as they are', so we can solve our problems in clinging on them; therefore, our mind would free from the eternally changing of phenomenon.

'Awareness of self' - Awareness of the Body and its Movements

Also, the Buddha has often reminded us pays much attention to the realization of the Body to its movements and

---

[1] Ibid, p.88-89

the processes taking place in it. Many processes in our body are taking their place without our attention and awareness: for example, many people have a habit of nervously biting their nails, or clicking with their joints, or winding long hair on the fingers at every turn; such things are considered some kind of a stress level indicators. They are usually referred to neurotic disorders that often caused by stress. And, as it known, the first step to treat such diseases is to diagnose them.

However, this things are just floating on the surface; if we look a little deeper, we will undoubtedly realize that there is a huge amount of actions and processes in our bodies eluding our attention: we always fall asleep and wake up, we eat food and we drink, we blink with our eyes, we breathe, and our internal organs are working without interruption. In such case, we have to train our mind in perceiving both internal and external worlds.[1]

The best way to aware our body is meditation practicing because it is much easier obtained when the body and mind are fully relaxed. However, this should not be limited only with meditations, it is necessary to try ourselves in awareness using every movement of our bodies, focusing on each individual case, as much as possible. The Buddha says: 'he remains focused internally on the body in & of itself, or externally on the body in & of itself, or both internally & externally on the body in & of itself. Or he remains focused on the phenomenon of origination with regard to the body, on the phenomenon of passing away with regard to the body, or on the phenomenon of origination & passing away with regard to the body. Or his mindfulness that 'There is a body' is maintained to the extent of knowledge & remembrance. And he remains independent, and unsustained by (not clinging to) anything in the world. This is how a monk

---

[1] Ibid, p.89-91

remains focused on the body in & of itself"[1], and then he also gives more specific guidances, saying that everyone should be aware of the position of his body, for example when sitting or lying down. It is necessary to strive for the awareness of every process in our bodies, as when we eat, or when chew it, just when we looking back on the street. More simply, the movement of each and every muscle in the body should be aware of.

Nevertheless, this is only the most obvious things. It seems to be impossible to understand all processes inside of us, without realizing of what causes them. Thus, to appreciate our bodies, we have to know of which parts they composed at least. As the understanding and close relationship with our own bodies allows us to understand the people and nature around us at a much higher quality level, and then suddenly would allow us to interact more productively with the entire world. This also applies in the reverse order - watching other people, we can better understand ourselves because many things are visible only in this way.

'Awareness of Feelings'

The awareness of the feelings takes no less importance because being aware of sensory reactions of the organism to help us in achieving skilful emotional states. The Buddha greatly simplifies the determination of the senses, and highlighting the most important criteria: 'painful feelings', 'pleasant feelings' and 'neither-painful-nor-pleasant feelings'; the manifestation of each of them has more important characteristics: 'of the flesh (carnality)' and 'not of the flesh' as well.

Following the manifestations of our feelings and emotions, we could learn to control them, becoming less dependent on

---

[1] DN 22, Maha-satipatthana Sutta: The Great Frames of Reference

factors of the external world, constantly distracting us. Such way of controlling feelings also helps us to track the causes of negative 'painful feelings' and 'pleasant feelings' and to get rid of them gradually.

The negative 'painful feelings' and 'pleasant feelings' of carnality: for example, feeling of happiness when putting our back on a newly purchased bed, and feeling of sadness when the bed no longer beauty and softness, or feeling very light when we drink, and feeling depressed when we drink too much. The positive 'painful feelings' and 'pleasant feelings' not of carnality: for example, feeling of peacefulness when our mind is less afflictions, or meditating in a quiet place, and feeling sad when we see someone oppressed by others etc ...

'Awareness of Thought'

The thinking process of an average person has no direction. Oftenly, thoughts seem to come from fiction, then creating constant noise in head. The brain of present-day human used to take a huge amount of information coming from all sides. We often do not even realize that this noise could force us to think about anything.

Before we perceive any kind of information, it extends through many 'filters' consisting of our beliefs, knowledge, experience, and of course, of the other opinions-many of whom are hardly trying to impose on us their vision of the situation. In more plain words, it works as censorship, but on a much deeper level. It happens very often that we do not attach much importance to the fact of how many of these 'filters' our idea passed through previously. Of course, that raises a lot of questions of the following type: 'whether it is our thoughts at all?'; 'Is it our reactions?'; 'Whether our desires are real?'; 'And whether it is our solutions?'; 'Or they imposed by someone or something from outside?' (Sangharakshita)

Understanding of such things is clearly what the 'awareness of thought' is helping to figure out our positive thought.

'Awareness of People'

The interaction with other people is very important for Buddhism; another important component part of the 'right mindfulness' is an awareness of other people. Oftenly, other people are perceived by us, as a kind of external objects that just have more features compared to the other objects. It is often difficult for us to imagine that every person on the Earth planet just thinks and feels in almost same way; everyone has his or her own feelings and needs, plans and ideas, fears and passions, which were based on the same principles from over the ages. As mentioned above, 'awareness of people' will help to establish communication, transferring it to a new level and completely inaccessible without doing it. Seeking and reaching such understanding of each other will make people being able to communicate on a truly new level, providing better support to each other, to cease any provoking of unnecessary conflicts, and avoiding any misunderstandings.

'Awareness of Reality'

The fourth and last level of awareness, where people can stay at, and which the Buddha's teachings lead us to - is the 'awareness of reality'. As it can be seen from above, each of these levels requires more and more complex processes leading to the full 'right mindfulness'. As the first step required awareness of material objects, of nature that surrounds us, and all the things that we have somehow come across. The second step requires much more efforts - to understand ourselves as creatures that are made of flesh and blood, but at the same time has the ability to think and feel. The third step requires us to awareness of others - expanding the scope defined by the first two levels (Sangharakshita). The fourth level - 'awareness of reality' is considered the most difficult to achieve because it brings together three previous, more expanding them, spreading the awareness on the whole Reality, awareness of each individual part of this reality, and of each their interactions.

"In Buddhism, practicing Mindfulness of reality is awareness of what to be here, and we can select any minful object for ourselves. We can observe a flower, clouds or our breath. The energy of mindfulness involves concentrate energy. When mindfulness and concentration have strength enought, we have the vision of wisdom. "We understood the nature of what is here; we breakthroug into the nature of reality."[1] Awareness is what right here, and right now that not on wishful thinking or future dreams. The Mindfulness is embracing reality, and reality is no longer divided by duality, and birth and death are seen in the interrelated ongoing.

In addition, the oftenly practices of Mindfulness have more beneficial effects to health. A new study by scientists in Wisconsin, Spain, and France reported the first evidence of specific molecular changes in the body after a period of mindful practicing.

The study examined the effects of a day of intensive mindfulness practice in a group of experienced meditators, and compared to a group of unexperienced subjects. After eight hours of mindfulness practice, the meditators showed a wide range of differences in genes and molecules, including altered levels of gene-regulating machinery and reduced levels of pro-inflammatory genes, which correlated with the physical recovery faster from a stressful situation.

"To the best of our knowledge, this is the first paper that shows rapid alterations in gene expression within subjects

---

[1] Thich Nhat Hanh, *Body and Mind Are One*

associated with mindfulness meditation practice." (Richard J. Davidson)

"Most interestingly, the changes were observed in genes that are the current targets of anti-inflammatory and analgesic drugs." (Perla Kaliman) - The study was published in the Journal Psychoneuroendocrinology.

The Mindfulness is capable of healing the mind and body; when Mindfulness is present, reality is realized in the dependent arising, not bound by dogmatic thinking, or clouded by ego. At here the door began to open freely.

6.8 RIGHT CONCENTRATION (samyak-samādhi/sammā-samādhi)

"Now what, monks, is noble right concentration with its supports and requisite conditions? Any singleness of mind equipped with these seven factors - right view, right resolve, right speech, right action, right livelihood, right effort, and right mindfulness - is called noble right concentration with its supports & requisite conditions."[1]

The final stage of eightfold path called 'Right concentration' (samyak-samādhi / sammā-samādhi) as well as previous step; it also applies to the meditation division. As a final step towards Nirvana, the concentration gives a more practical guidance in meditation, not really giving us any further instructions, or any description of what it would be like at the end of eightfold pass. This makes the eightfold path complete because as a matter of fact, the only higher stage is Nirvana. On the other hand, such way of presentation of facts, coupled with the difficulties of translation, and due to the fact that the followers of the Buddha are divided into many sects; each of which has its own interpretations of

---

[1] MN 117, Maha-cattarisaka Sutta: The Great Forty

the Buddha's words, thus often appear two most popular interpretations.

The first one of them asserts that 'samādhi' should be understood as typical for Buddhists being concentration of the mind-practiced during meditations. The second version says that the word 'samādhi' refers to the state of a conditional dwelling in the Absolute Reality as close as possible to the Enlightenment. And of course, there is an option, which involves the usage of both interpretations at the same time that I think is much closer to the truth. Following that, the first term which is referring to the concentration of the mind called 'samatha'; the second one, which means the top of the Eightfold Path - 'samadhi', and between them as a link, there is the concept of attainments-called 'samapatti'. As such, the 'right concentration' contains as the aim, and the means of achieving it.

'Samatha' as the first of those three parts, it implies the first of all means 'repose'. This state of mind is typical for meditation when the mind is focused on the only one thing, and discarding any external stress. Thus, 'samatha' closely linked with 'four jhanas'-actually matching it. In addition, 'samatha' can also be divided into 3 stages-each of which is more difficult than the previous one. If the first stage seems to be quite simple, the only thing we have to do is to focus our attention on some material objects. The second phase is much more difficult since it is necessary to recreate focus on the 'twin' of the material object in our brain, such as practice of moving attention away from the real image to our inner projection of it is required in order to get rid of any details of extra sensory perceptions, and get the best out-just concentrating on the present moment. At the final stage of 'samatha', due to the intensity of concentration and absence of any distracting things, a person becomes fully merged with the image, and totally reunites with it.

'Samapatti' - People practice meditations and train their mind in concentration; they could experience some strange feelings, spiritual experiences, each of which produces a special appearance, as a kind of fleeting touch of the 'Enlightenment'. Manifestations of these things are very individual from person to person. The difference composed not only in type and in form of experience, not only in its frequency and duration, but also in its ability to affect on a person's life. In fact, it can happen in any manner: for example, the vision of blinding, all-consuming light, or vice versa - colorful geometric shapes and beautiful designs in all shapes and colors; people can hear a variety of sounds or smells. However, it is rather a vain attempt to explain the unprecedented influx of emotions as far as such impressions are very difficult to verbalize. At the same time, few effects are mostly common at 'samapatti' experiences: in this state, the person feels strong euphoria and joy, as is faced with something of a higher level of understanding (Sangharakshita).

Descriptions of similar feelings are common in today's counter-culture where they are called "mystical experience"- referring to the experiences obtained during the use of various psychedelic drugs such as LSD. Many people who advocated for the legalization of LSD in the 60s and later (most famous of them are Timothy Francis Leary, Ken Elton Kesey, Aldous Leonard Huxley) left descriptions of their own experiences, which ones, if we look closer, are very similar to the descriptions of 'samapatti'. Those of them who were also interested in Buddhism, also notices this similarity, stating that the use of psychedelics can give a person the same as a continuous meditation in conjunction with the following the path of Buddha. However, we should not forget that the 'samapatti' is the second step, which is in its essence consists of many small (relative to the final enlightenment) achievements, which are just like fragment pieces of the puzzle, and without reference to the other items on the Buddha's teachings; these achievements are not even closely such significant, as it is important not only to reach them; it is important to be prepared, and perceiving them at a different level of consciousness. Thus, if a person is not ready for practice of insight physically or mentally, it can seriously harm, only increasing fears, desires and passion.

Samadhi can be literally translated as 'concentration'. This state of mind is achieved through high meditative practice that calms the mind and gathers it in unity. It is necessary for the development of true wisdom, which comes at the process of a direct experience, direct knowledge, which is opposed to intellectual one-in the form of concepts and ideas.

The 'samadhi' in this context means a state of enlightenment mind; it is quite difficult to explain its sense to a person who previously was not interested in such things at all. In addition, the state of enlightenment itself, it's a whole different level of being, thinking and feeling, which is much higher than the ones we are used to; hence, it is no precise description ready for people to link to it (because Buddha teaches us how to reach enlightenment, not trying to give a specific description to it). On this basis, it would be more than just say that 'samadhi' is much more different from the usual life course of a modern man. In this case it was more convenient to use a method of denial for a better explanation. Thus, the most common description is the negation of the following three things: desire, ignorance and conditionality of existence. Accordingly, in this state, there is no signal of these feelings and affections maintaining in human mind; we can tell it is a feeling of complete freedom (Sangharakshita).

In addition, it is believed that the "Samadhi" state can be divided into three aspects.

'The Imageless Samadhi'

The first of 'animitta' samadhi, which means a state of complete freedom from any whatsoever images, such as thoughts and understanding that might distract. . "There is the case where with the complete transcending of perceptions of form, with the disappearance of perceptions of resistance, and not heeding perceptions of diversity; (perceiving) 'Infinite space', one... remains in the dimension of the infinitude of space: this is one way of being percipient when not sensitive to that dimension."[1]

'The Directionless Samadhi'

The second allocated aspect is 'appanihita' samadhi, which is often interpreted as a 'lack of direction', referring to the lack of need to move, no selfish desires, and in the full balance state. Moreover, it is worth noting that the lack of direction can also mean a complete fusion with the universe. "Further, with the complete transcending of the dimension of the infinitude of space, (perceiving) 'Infinite consciousness,' one... remains in the dimension of the infinitude of consciousness: this is another way of being percipient when not sensitive to that dimension."[2]

'The Samadhi of the Voidness'

The last aspect of samadhi is 'sunnata' - means emptines. However, the 'emptiness' appears here not in the usual context, but meaning the absence of everything. Rather, it is the presence and full knowledge of all areas of life-the highest stage of comprehension of life; it is beyond the limits

---

[1] AN 9.37, Ānanda sutta - With Ananda

[2] Ibid...

of the concepts, thinking or common senses: 'Further, with the complete transcending of the dimension of the infinitude of consciousness, (perceiving) "There is nothing', one... remains in the dimension of nothingness: this is another way of being percipient when not sensitive to that dimension."[1]

Refusing to own desires, refusing to value judgments, and observing life and spirituality to an awareness of correlate and no-self nature, people often come to the conclusion that everything in this world has the same qualities, being equal to significance and equal to insignificance.

However, refusing of the finite values to be entered into the infinite emptiness, and realizing equal dignity of all phenomena, one must follow the specific processes in the practice. Going past the dualistic categories of happiness and sadness, in a state of undistracted, the Right Concentration can be considered as complete.

The following in Saccavibhanga Sutta describes about the steps of Right concentration:

And what is right concentration?

[i] Here, the monk, detached from sense-desires, detached from unwholesome states, enters and remains in the first jhana (Sanskrit: dhyāna), in which there is applied and sustained thinking, together with joy and pleasure born of detachment.

[ii] And through the subsiding of applied and sustained thinking, with the gaining of inner stillness and oneness of mind, he enters and remains in the second jhana, which is without applied and sustained thinking, and in which there are joy and pleasure born of concentration.

---

[1] Ibid...

[iii] And through the fading of joy, he remains equanimous, mindful and aware, and he experiences in his body the pleasure of which the Noble Ones say: "equanimous, mindful and dwelling in pleasure", and thus he enters and remains in the third jhana.

[iv] And through the giving up of pleasure and pain, and through the previous disappearance of happiness and sadness, he enters and remains in the fourth jhana, which is without pleasure and pain, and in which there is pure equanimity and mindfulness.

This is called right concentration.[1]

In conclusion, the Right Concentration is deeply practice in meditation. it is a process through the seven stages of the Eightfold Path, in which the continuous effort to maintain mindfulness in all situations. In the completely pure state of Right concentration, also known as Nirvana state. However, for those practitioners are more busy in their daily lives, they can do it by practice mindfulness, observing their actions in awareness, and seeing the phenomenon of mind and circumstances in the present moment. To this frequent awakening, not just gradually purging negative thoughts, but positive thoughts will develop better-creating unexpected opportunities for inner enlightenment at a certain time to themselve, and the fruit of this enlightenment have more practical values to share with others. This is also a Buddha's reminder: "Change your thoughts, and you can change the world."

---

[1] Roderick Bucknell, Chris Kang, The Meditative Way: Readings in the Theory and Practice of Buddhist Meditation. Routledge .p.12-13

7. PRACTICING BUDDHISM IN ALL SPHERES OF LIFE AS A WAY TO ACHIEVE COMPASSION AND WISDOM IN A NEW WOLD

7.1 IN EVERYDAY LIFE

Having discussed the Noble Eightfold Path, we now can see further how its instructions from the Buddhist point of view, which should be followed so that our world became a better place. But life is very diverse, and we often cannot ever realize that we are making something against those instructions, and this deed or thought sooner or later will become harmful to you or other people. Our sight is often faded by the state we are in and we cannot recognize the three poisons of greed, hatred and delusion from ours deviant thoughts that faded our wisdom. For that reason to a resolution of this thesis in the following chapter, I will discuss how Buddha's teaching can change different elements of our lives.

The Buddhists believe that to practice the teaching, it is not necessarily to sit for hours in the lotus position, wearing exotic oriental clothes, or recite mantras. Dharma practice can be carried out in everyday life. In their view, the practice of Buddhism is not so much in a prayer but in the nature of communication with the people around you and as in the thoughts with which you take up any job. The word 'dharma' in some way means a protective method. This is what we do to avoid the problems. Practice of dharmas or the Buddhist teaching is specifically aimed at eliminating the problems by perfecting our mind and the development of compassion.

How can the development of compassion actually

eliminate the negative issues? Buddhism teaches that every man who is being angry and hatred, at the same time, he is giving offense by words or even making a real harm that is faded with depressions of the mind. In the fact, the depressions arises from his dissatisfaction, and he is hoping with the help of the backbiting or bad deeds to ease this state to become a little bit happier. He is envious with everyone who looks more calm and happier than he is himself. This is understandable that in such a way as a deluded man is unlikely to achieve happiness, and that is why, in a Buddhist point of view, he deserves compassion.

After all, in everyone who was born a man, or a living being ingeneral, there is a nature of the Buddha (Tathagatagarbha) - enlightenment or frequent awakening. A lot of problems that occur in everyday life because we are chasing delusions, loss of awareness, so anger often employed inside our minds. The anger should be aimed not at someone who is being deluded, but one the delusion itself, which makes this someone unhappy and encourages to hurt other living beings. We can compare such defilement to the evil man who picked up a stick and hit the dog. Inexperienced dog may be angry at the stick, and even bite it up until it guesses that the real harm comes from the one who holds the stick. The same goes with anger: do not get angry with the person who expresses it: he, in this case, is like a stick in the hands of an evil man - a weapon 'in the hands' of his defilement.[1]

On the contrary, we must start compassionate heart to person who is angry in hurtful words to you: because such a behavior means that he or she is unhappy. According to the Dalai Lama, although people are great and friendly or unattractive and troublesome, ultimately they are human

---

[1] Nanasampanno, Acariya Maha Boowa, Things As They Are

beings, just like you, they want happiness and do not want suffering. Moreover, their right to overcome suffering and be happy is equal like you. Now, when you realize that all beings are equal in their desire for happiness and their rights in order to achieve this, you will automatically receive the sympathy and closeness to them. Through accustoming with your mind, with the consciousness of the whole altruism, you develop a feeling of responsibility for others: the wish to actively help them overcome problems. Nor is this wish selective; it applies equally to all. As long they are human beings experiencing pleasure and pain like you, there is no reasonable basis to discriminate between them or to change your concern to them if they behave negatively.[1] This will be an excellent practice of Dharma in daily life.

Whether someone offends you intentionally or accidentally, as Buddhist teachers say, you should mentally thank this person because he or she has just given you a good reason to train in the practice of Buddhist teaching. If you resist and do not take offense, you cannot experience a great joy of having done one more step on the path of Dharma. If you break out with irritation in response, then people would simply find your weak spo and hurt your feelings and awakened your pride. In this case, from Buddhist viewpoint, you should remember this case and work with it.

Explaining what it means to practice Buddhism in daily life, Alexander Berzin defines it the following way: When we have problems, we turn inwards, trying to find their source inside us, and as soon as we have defined it; we try to change the situation from within. The main, the deepest cause of our problems within us is our own attitudes, especially our confusion. However, Berzin warns us that turning inwards in

---

[1] The fourteenth Dalai Lama, *Compassion and the Individual*

searching a root of a certain problem does not imply a moral judgment on how good or bad person we are. Also, there is no sense in this self-blame or self-praise. We just need to figure out where is the root cause of our suffering, and eliminate it and become happier.[1]

The help to other living beings is also the practice of Dharma; which is a necessary virtue in daily basis to Buddhists. The Buddha said: "Be kind to all creatures; this is the true religion." To start, we try to practice the help of our loved ones first, and after people all around us; for example, if the husband locked himself in a room to read book, and his wife was washing the dishes or cooking for the whole family with her happiness, in this case, his wife would be a much better Buddhist than his husband. So, there is no point in the many hours of praying and doing specific practices if our efforts do not manifest themselves by helping other simply in our daily life.

To Buddhist adherents, the occasion to practice the Dharma can be any situation of life. If you are standing in a traffic jam - instead of being irritated, you can recite the mantra or keep mindfulness of your breathing, so your mind wouldn't longer worry about waiting for the road would quickly clear, and all the members of the movement could continue their journey. Driving on public transport, you have an opportunity to practice patience and compassion. Do you concede the sitting place when you are tired yourself? Do you feel angry those who pushed you? What are your thoughts during a long journey? The teachers of Buddhism urge all of us to think about it.

Buddhism thinks that it is not necessary to separate religious practices and real life; for laity the events that occur

---

[1] Berzin, Alexander. "Anger: Dealing with Disturbing Emotions."

around them is the best school of Buddhism. If you get sick and have to stay in bed, facing death, you can also use this time to reflect on your life, such as having prayer, raise the awareness, and contemplate of your distresses and realms that you will go to. Pende Hawter shows in "Death and Dying in the Tibetan Buddhist Tradition" that: "Contemplation and meditation on death and impermanence are regarded as very important in Buddhism for two reasons: (1) it is only by recognizing how precious and how short life is that we are most likely to make it meaningful and to live it fully and (2) by understanding the death process and familiarizing ourselves with it, we can remove fear at the time of death and ensure a good rebirth.

Because the way in which we live our lives and our state of mind at death directly influence our future lives, it is said that the aim or mark of a spiritual practitioner is to have no fear or regrets at the time of death. People who practice to the best of their abilities will die; it is said in a state of great bliss. The mediocre practitioner will die happily. Even the initial practitioner will have neither fear nor dread at the time of death, so one should aim at achieving at least the smallest of these results.

There are two common meditations on death in the Tibetan tradition. The first looks at the certainty and imminence of death and what will be of benefit at the time of death in order to motivate us to make the best use of our lives. The second is a simulation or rehearsal of the actual death process, which familiarizes us with death and takes away the fear of the unknown, thus allowing us to die skillfully. Traditionally, in Buddhist countries, one is also encouraged to go to a cemetery or burial ground to contemplate on death and become familiar with this inevitable event.

The first of these meditations is known as the nine-round death meditation, in which we contemplate the three roots, the nine reasons, and the three convictions, as described below:

A. Death is certain

1. There is no possible way to escape death. No-one ever has, not even Jesus, Buddha, etc. Of the current world population of over 5 billion people, almost none will be alive in 100 years time.

2. Life has a definite, inflexible limit and each moment brings us closer to the finality of this life. We are dying from the moment we are born.

3. Death comes in a moment and its time is unexpected. All that separates us from the next life is one breath.

Conviction: To practice the spiritual path and ripen our inner potential by cultivating positive mental qualities and abandoning disturbing mental qualities.

B. The time of death is uncertain

4. The duration of our lifespan is uncertain. The young can die before the old, the healthy before the sick, etc.

5. There are many causes and circumstances that lead to death but few that favour the sustenance of life. Even things that sustain life can kill us, for example food, motor vehicles, property.

6. The weakness and fragility of one's physical body contribute to life's uncertainty. The body can be easily destroyed by disease or accident, for example cancer, AIDS, vehicle accidents, other disasters.

Conviction: To ripen our inner potential now, without delay.

C. The only thing that can help us at the time of death is our mental/spiritual developments

(Because all that goes on to the next life is our mind with its karmic (positive or negative) imprints.)

7. Worldly possessions such as wealth, position, money can't help

8. Relatives and friends can neither prevent death nor go with us.

9. Even our own precious body is of no help to us. We have to leave it behind like a shell, an empty husk, an overcoat.

Conviction: To ripen our inner potential purely, without staining our efforts with attachment to worldly concerns..."[1]

Contemplating the actual death process is very important because advanced practitioners can engage in a series of yogas that are modeled on death and rebirth until they gain such control over them that they are no longer subject to ordinary uncontrolled death and rebirth.

Love - family is another vast field of opportunities to learn something to become more patient, supportive and compassionate. You just have no be afraid to open your heart, to be grateful for all the goods in the difficult moments, and to better understand the good qualities of your life partner or others. Loving and taking full responsibility with your wife (husband) and your children is a noble qualities that a Buddhist should be done.

Communication with elderly parents or other relatives is another example of such a situation. In our time, it has become almost fashionable to blame the parents for not doing something for us earlier or for doing something wrong. Many

---

[1] Ven. Pende Hawter, "Death and Dying in the Tibetan Buddhist Tradition"

even see the meaning of the currently developing theories of psychotherapy and psychoanalysis as to blame their parents: they say, they were not loved in their childhood, and poorly cared for and that became the cause of all their complexes in the adult life. Nevertheless, people who think in such a way, according to the convictions of the Buddhist, without the fact that psychotherapy, as well as Buddhism says that every adult has a responsibility for his own life. Perhaps someone forgot the priceless gifts that his or her parents giving to him or her. You should be thankful to them at least for the fact that you were born, and in addition, they have fed you and clothed you, gave you the knowledge of the world, and so on. Further be grateful for the parents, the Buddhists also have to know how to repay the debt they owe their parents in an ethical way. The Buddha explains what we should repay the debt we owe our parents:

"I tell you, monks, there are two people who are not easy to repay. Which two? Your mother & father.

"Even if you were to carry your mother on one shoulder & your father on the other shoulder for 100 years, and were to look after them by anointing, massaging, bathing, & rubbing their limbs, and they were to defecate & urinate right there [on your shoulders], you would not in that way pay or repay your parents. If you were to establish your mother & father in absolute sovereignty over this great earth, abounding in the seven treasures, you would not in that way pay or repay your parents.

"Why is that? Mother & father did much for their children. They care for them, they nourish them, and they introduce them to this world. But anyone who rouses his unbelieving mother & father, settles & establishes them in conviction; rouses his unvirtuous mother & father, settles & establishes them in virtue; rouses his stingy mother & father, settles &

establishes them in generosity; rouses his foolish mother & father, settles & establishes them in discernment: To this extent one pays & repays one's mother & father."[1]

Perhaps they were not perfect but they certainly tried as best they could. For the Buddhists, the persons themselves are responsible for what happens in their lives, for the formation of their characters and all of their problems:

> *"By oneself is evil done,*
> *by oneself defiled,*
> *by oneself it's left undone,*
> *by self alone one purified.*
> *Purity, impurity on oneself depend,*
> *no one can purify another."[2]*

(Attana hi kataj papaj
Attana savkilissati
Attana akataj papaj
Attana va visujjhati
Suddhi asuddhi paccattaj
N'abbo abbaj visodhaye.)

In our daily life, if we are aware that all of problems come from ourselves, we will have sympathy and love easier for the people around us.

7.2 THE PROBLEMS IN SOCIAL LIFE

The most fundamental social structure is marriage. Marriage is a social agreement or institution established by people for the sake of their personal well-being and happiness. This institution has function to maintain harmony and order in the process of procreation, and by that distinguishes

---

[1] AN 2.31-32, Bhikkhu-Kataññu Suttas

[2] DhP165/Translated by Ven. Weragoda Sarada Maha Thero

human society from animals. Although nothing is said so much in the Buddhist texts on the subject of monogamy and polygamy, secular followers are advised to be limited to one spouse. The Buddha did not make any rules for a married life, but he gave some recommendations concerning how to make a married life happier. In his sermons, many things indicate that it is much wiser, better and easier to be faithful to one spouse, not to hurt someone's feelings and not to take an interest in other partners.[1]

The Buddha's teaching says that one of the profound reasons for the downfall of man is loving relationships with other women. Here it is obviously implied that the woman if coming into love affairs with several men, she also has to suffer. One has to realize the difficulties, trials and tribulations which she has to go through just to maintain family life. It could be increased by several times if you encounter them on the background of the additional difficulties created by yourselves. Understanding the human weakness, the Buddha's one of the rules taught followers to restrain from the sexual misconduct and debauchery. The third of the Five Precepts undertaken by lay Buddhists runs: Kamesu micchacara veramani sikkhapadam samadiyami, "I undertake the course of training in refraining from wrong-doing in respect of sensuality."

View of Buddhism at marriage like the society under democracy is very liberal: marriage is a private matter - not a duty which imposed by religion. In Buddhism, there is no rule persuading a person to marry, remain single, or live in ultimate celibacy. There are no such rules which require Buddhists to have children or to refraing from having children, or to limit the number of children. Buddhism gives

---

[1] Ven. K. Sri Dhammananda, "A Happy Married Life"

each human being a freedom to decide on their own issues all related to marriage.

Then a question arises: why Buddhist monks and nuns refrain from marriage if there are no direct instructions in a relation to marriage? The main reason is that the monks and nuns have chosen a lifestyle which purpose is liberation for themselves and serving people; celibacy is a part of this lifestyle. Those who renounced worldly life - voluntarily renounce family ties to have no worldly personal duties in order to maintain peace of mind. They want to completely dedicate their lives to the service to others and to achieve their spiritual liberation. In today's society, even though Buddhist monks do not conduct the marriage ceremonies for Buddhists, they may be invited to perform certain religious rituals in order to bless the betrothed couple. The same can be performed by Buddhist nuns.[1]

To sex without marriage is also a problem of today's society. Containment or the restriction of desires is the first principle of any civilization, including our today's society. But along with that, we have contaminated the sexual atmosphere around us and through the media over-exaggerated the need of the body and mind in a sexual satisfaction. As a result of exploitation of sexual desire by some hidden forces of society, today's young people have formed such an attitude to sex that they minds are totally eclipsed by the hindrances, and sexual desire is never satisfied; The Buddha said: "People have much desires and find the ways to satisfy their desires as same as the ones who get leprosy just like scratching your itch." And the result is more suffering.

In a human life, sexual relationships should take their particular place, and here, from the Buddhist point of view,

---

[1] Ibid...

any unnatural limitations or unhealthy inflations should not be allowed. Sex must also be controlled by a will, and it is possible, if you treat it wisely and give it a proper place in life. In contrast to what a modern society is trying to impress upon us, sex should not be considered to be the most important part of a happy married life. Those who abuse their own pleasures can become slaves of sexual tension, and in the end that will destroy the love and respect in marriage. As in every other sphere, Buddhists recommend to stick to moderation and rationality in sexual needs.[1]

Marriage is a bond of a commonwealth in which a man and woman vow to enter together for a whole life. The three main principles on which a married couple should be built and grown are patience, tolerance and understanding while love should be the node that connects partners to each other to maintain a happy family-the material conditions are needed as well. A sign of a good marriage is the word 'ours' rather than 'yours' or 'mine'. The partners in a good couple should open their hearts to each other and have no secrets. When there are secrets, it creates a suspicion, and the suspicion is an element that can destroy love in any marriage union before. The Suspicion also breeds jealousy, the jealousy generates anger, the anger creates hatred, the hatred turns into hostility, and the hostility may result in a greater suffering like bloodshed, suicide or even murder.[2]

A happy marriage is built on the foundation of love, loyalty, and responsibility. The Buddha taught a husband must love and respect his wife, not commit adultery, telling his wife where he go outside, providing clothings, jewelry for his wife, and he indoor assets were entrusted to his wife.

---

[1] Ibid...

[2] Ibid...

And a wife was owed her husband's respect, courtesy and faithfulness. Further, a wife was to be given authority in the home and provided with adornments. A wife is obligated to perform her duties well, discharging them skillfully and industriously. She is to be faithful to her husband and to be hospitable to friends and relations. And she should "protect what he brings," which suggests taking care of whatever her husband provides her.[1]

Separation or divorce is also not prohibited in Buddhism although the need for it would be extremely rare if the spouses strictly followed the instructions of the Buddha. Men and women are absolutely free to leave if they cannot reach a mutual agreement. It is better to separate than for a long time to lead a family life suffered by yourself, your wife and your children (Dhammananda). Also, the Buddha advises older men to not marry young women because an old man and a young wife are highly unlikely to be compatible, and that can trigger unnecessary difficulties, disharmony and downfall.[2]

Society is growing due to the web of relationships that are intertwined and interdependent. Each connection between people is a sincere dedication to the promotion and protection of other members of community or group. Marriage plays an essential role on this complicated web of relations which provided such support and protection. From a Buddhist point of view, a good marriage should grow and develop consistently by understanding, but not by impulse, from true devotion, but not from mere indulgence. The institution of marriage provides a strong fundament for a development of culture with a beautiful community of two people supporting

---

[1] DN 31, Sigalovada Sutta: The Buddha's Advice to Sigalaka

[2] Sn 1.6, Parabhava Sutta: Discourse on Downfall

each other and avoiding loneliness, fear and deprivation together. In marriage, each spouse is trying to complement the other; it aims at giving courage and strength to show support, recognize, as well as appreciate the ability of the other partner. In couple life, there does not appear thinking about who is more important. The other complement is in equal partnership, radiating gentleness, self-control, mutual respect, generosity, equanimity and devotion.

Other importance in marriage to Buddhists is to have no reason to object to the measures for the prevention of pregnancy. They are free to use both old and modern contraceptives. Those who oppose contraception and argue that the use of this prevent way is contrary to God's law that must understand that this view is in no way justified. Measures to prevent pregnancy are intended to prevent the emergence of a new living being. In this care, the killing does not occur and unskillful action (akusala kamma) is not performed. However, if people commit any act aimed at the commission of an abortion, this act is considered to be bad kamma because abortion is a deprivation of life of visible or invisible creatures. For that reason, Buddhists are in compliance with the first of five precepts, so there is no excuse for abortion.

The Buddha's teaching states that the act of deliberate murder is committed in compliance with the five conditions. These conditions are following: the presence of a living being, the knowledge or awareness of (the killer) that this creature is a living, the intention to commit murder, making an effort to kill, and death of a living being in the result of this effort.[1]

At the moment of conception, the living entity is emerged, and thus it satisfies the first condition in the womb. A few

---

[1] Ven. K. Sri Dhammananda, "A Happy Married Life"

months later, the mother realizes that within her there is a new life, and thus it satisfies the second condition. Then, for one reason or another she wishes to get rid of this living being located in her womb. So she starts searching for a doctor to have an abortion, and it satisfies the third condition. When a doctor makes the operation, the fourth condition is satisfied, and in which a living being dies; thus, all the five conditions are satisfied. The result has been a violation of the first rule, which teaches to refrain from taking life, so this action of abortion is equivalent to killing a person. With regard to measures for the prevention of pregnancy, there is the opposite situation: a living entity in this case does not appear, so that all five conditions are not satisfied (Dhammananda). According to the Buddhist doctrine, we have no reason to say that we have the right only to take the life of a creature when it has already emerged.

In some situations, people assume that they are forced to make this for the sake of their own convenience. But we should not justify an abortion because one way or another they will have to face bad consequences. In some countries, abortion is legal, but it is done simply in order to overcome social problems. Buddhism teaches not to neglect the moral principles for the sake of convenience of the people. These principles serve as a good of all mankind.

Another acute social problem is suicide. Deprivation of life of oneself in all circumstances is erroneous act from both ethical and spiritual point of view. Depriving oneself of life because of the failures and frustration only increases the suffering. Suicide is a cowardly way to deal with the life problems. In any bad circumstance, person cannot commit a method of suicide if his mind is calm and pure. If someone leaves this world in a state of confusion and frustration, it is very unlikely that he will be reborn in the better conditions.

Such an exit from life is a bad or unskillful act since it is provoked by the mind filled with selfishness, greed, hatred, and most importantly defilement. Those people who commit suicide presumably have not learned to perceive their problems, and understand the truth of life and use the ability to think properly. Such people are unable "to understand the essence of the life and the conditions of the world in which they live."[1]

Some sacrifice their lives for a reason, which they consider as good and noble. They deprive themselves of life by committing self-immolation, using firearms or fasting. Such actions someone can call bold and brave; but from the Buddhist point of view, it cannot be approved. The Buddha clearly explained that the state of consciousness that lead to suicide, only lead to more suffering. Such a holistic position again proves how positive and life-affirming worldview is Buddhism.[2]

To affirm optimistically life, we need to face the negative issues, aware of their roots, and to find the ways to overcome. According to Buddhism, we were born as a human living is a precious opportunity, so should appreciate to ourselves; in addition, we also have to know how to create good karma for the present and future. Identifying the negative causes making suffering comes from our desires, we would have proper awareness to our body and mind, and the external situation in a more positive direction.

> *"The cause of all suffering*
> *Is rooted in desire*
> *If desire be extinguished,*
> *Suffering has no foothold."*[3]

---

[1] Ibid...

[2] Ibid...

[3] The Threefold Lotus Sutra, 101

Therefore, the pain is not outside but inside us. The problems of human and society will be resolved when every person reduces his or her desires by realizing the suffering and its causes, and knowing how to transform all of life's problems in a truly peaceful state of mind.

Live in Joy, in love,
Even among those who hate.
Live in joy, in health,
Even among the afflicted.
Live in joy, in peace,
Even among the troubled.
Look within. Be still.
Free from fear and attachment,
Know the sweet joy of living in the way.
(Dhammapada).

7.3 THE APPLICATION OF BUDDHIST ECONOMICS IN LIFE

As it known, today's global economics is experiencing a crisis, and showing and proving completely uselessness of economists, even capitalism. All global world relations are governed by the policy; this is one of its objectives. As historically, the level of economic development of countries is moving from east to west: Ancient Greece, the Roman Empire, England, and USA ... in the world capital and the global economy; the controls have always been in the hands of these territorial leaders. On this basis it would be logical to consider the theoretical possibility of the use of certain Buddhist principles in accordance with the economics. If earlier it was customary to assume that in fact the only option to enter the 'high society' was born within it, then after the beginning of the 20th century, and especially in modern time, many examples show us that, in fact, to one day become incredibly rich and famous all over the world can be anyone with some effort. Since then, many people from poor families earned their capital; it is thousands of businessmen, politicians, artists, musicians, actors, athletes, and so on.

The change from the poverty to the richness is not only depending on the change in the social structure; however, it also depends on the cognitive ability, morality and personal efforts as the main motivation. According to Buddhism, poverty is unhappy because it involves dukkha (suffering). The goal of the Buddha's teaching is to end sufferings, and want to stop sufferings we must find the cause of it first. Standing on the individual angel, poverty comes from the lack of education (a part of ignorance), laziness, profligate, drug addiction, or evil livehood... In social aspect, the poverty arises from greed, exploitation, and there is no disruptive between the rich man and the poor man; that is due to human' selfishness and insensitivity or a injustice of government that makes richness and poverty far away clearly.

The fact that in earlier times to become a head of state or to somehow good influence his fate could only be born in a rich or influential class, but do not forget that the government is also a great temptation which became the cornerstone and wayward than in the human world. Tasted and enjoyed the power, most of all they want to hold it in their hands. For this they went to the monstrous deeds, not only contrary to the principles of Buddhism but also often contradict global society (and his personal including) to the well-being and survival, such as determining the fate of many thousands of people. Thus, dividing humanity of the world in the interval from antiquity to the late nineteenth century in the conventional groups of rich and poor, and following the options of mutual movement between the castes in different societies, comparing similar data of the twentieth century and the twenty-first century, we find now the movement from one group to another is much easier than it has ever been. Thus, many young people have become hostages of the idea of power and money.

Power and money are considered the criteria of being happy; however, if we couldn't know how to use them in the spirit of ethics and wisdom, they become obstacles in our path. In addition to know how to use them, those who make a lot of assets but unknown how to share, donate and save their assets, such one cannot be called smart. Buddha explained ten behaviors following to promote ethical means of doing businessman or rich man, and show the ways to enjoy pleasure from one's wealth truly:

Consumers of sense-pleasure who acquire money by unscrupulous means (i.e. acquire wealth by wrong livelihood) and having acquired it derive no enjoyment from it, not do they disburse it for the benefit of others nor donate it for a meritorious cause. Such an attitude to wealth cannot be said to be smart - and on the contrary burdens them with worse demerit.

Consumers of sense pleasure who acquire money by unscrupulous means, but who derive enjoyment from it, but who don't disburse it for the benefit of others or donate it for meritorious causes. Such an attitude to wealth is not smart in the acquisition and not particularly smart in the spending - especially in the conservation of wealth; it is definitely not smart.

Consumers of sense-pleasure who acquire money by unscrupulous means but who derive enjoyment from their wealth, disburse their wealth for others, and donating it for meritorious causes too.

Consumers of sense-pleasure who acquire wealth by a mixture of scrupulous and unscrupulous means (wealth in this case might be acquired partly honestly by a salary, but the rest might come from bribes - i.e. both right and wrong livelihood) - but who derive no enjoyment from their wealth, don't disburse their wealth for others and don't donate it for meritorious causes. Such an attitude to wealth may or may not be smart in the acquisition and is definitely not smart in the spending and saving.

Consumers of sense-pleasure who acquire wealth by a mixture of scrupulous and unscrupulous means, who derive enjoyment from it, but fail to disburse it for the benefit of others or to donate it for meritorious causes. Such an attitude to wealth may or may not be smart in the acquisition, is reasonably smart in the spending, but not in the saving;

Consumers of sense-pleasure who acquire wealth by a mixture of scrupulous and unscrupulous means, who derive enjoyment from it and disburse it for the benefit of others and also donate it for meritorious causes. Such an attitude to wealth may or may not be smart in the acquisition, but which is smart in the usage and the saving.

Consumers of sense-pleasure who acquire money solely by scrupulous means (solely by right livelihood) but who derive no enjoyment from their wealth and neither disburse their wealth for the benefit of others nor donate it for meritorious causes. Such an attitude to wealth can be considered smart in the acquisition but not smart in the usage or the saving.

Consumers of sense-pleasure who acquire money solely by scrupulous means, who derive enjoyment from their wealth and but do not disburse their wealth for the benefit of others nor donate it for meritorious causes. Such an attitude to wealth can be considered smart in the acquisition and usage but not smart in the saving.

Consumers of sense-pleasure who acquire money solely by scrupulous means, who derive enjoyment from their wealth and also do disburse their wealth for the benefit of others and donate it for meritorious causes. However, in spite of all their good actions, the people of these categories remain blind to the harmfulness of sense-pleasure -- they lack the wisdom to be motivated to renounce sense-pleasure. Such an attitude to wealth can be considered smart in the acquisition, the usage and the saving but because such people lack insight into the harmfulness of sense pleasure, they lack the power to liberate themselves from the clutches of the defilements of sense-pleasure -- because they haven't had the chance to associate sufficiently with the wise.

Consumers of sense-pleasure who acquire money solely by scrupulous means, who derive pleasure from their wealth, who disburse their wealth for others and donate it for meritorious causes. In addition, those of this category are no longer blind to the harmfulness of sense-pleasure - thus they have the wisdom to want to escape from the cycle of existence [samsara] and this wisdom will allow them to renounce attachment to the use of the wealth. Such an attitude to wealth can be considered smart in the acquisition, the usage and the saving and furthermore allows one to overcome oneís defilements, ultimately to enter upon Nirvana.[1]

Such economic value in Buddhism is associated with quality of life, not just for oneself but for others. However, we determine the quality of life not only in terms of physical facilities, but also in terms of spiritual welfare, and finally the liberation of the mind from nagtive trends and depression in order to attain the ultimate ideal of freedom (Nirvana).

As we know, the western and eastern world philosophies have a lot of differences between them, one of which is the

---

[1] A.10_091, Kaamabhogii Sutta, those who enjoy sense pleasures

treatment of one of the seemingly basic concepts of existence - freedom. Freedom for the followers of Western philosophy is, first and foremost, freedom of action. In this sense, 'freedom' - it goes beyond, bursting the shackles, the possibility of impunity and gratuitous dreams, and constant pandering to his ego. Also by the desire and passion has always been the object of a taboo in the west, due to the strong influence of religion on public life, particularly noticeable was the case in the middle Ages and during the Inquisition, so they then formed the concept of the above-mentioned manner. According principles of Buddhism, the 'freedom' means by a just liberty from suffering caused by desire. Because of this we can assume that the differences between East and West can be derived from that concept.

Unconforming in popular thinking, the Buddha encouraged that "self-sufficient economy, maintaining morality" to the monks and nuns to renounce the negative desires which prevent freedom of mind. However, he also inspirited the wealth and social development for laities. In "Happiness appropriate to a householder" includes ownership [atthisukha], enjoyment [bhogasukha], getting rid from debt [ananasukha] and unmistakes [anavajjasukha]; In this sutra, the Buddha praised and encouraged to limit desires [appicchata] which causes grief. Nevertheless, the importance of a Buddhist, in the economic process for his income, saving or spending money, he should make sense to him and others. Once wealthy, we also use our properties for supporting the healthy goals in life - not squandering money without main purpose, or in any way leading to grow more of the negativity of the greed, hatred and delusion of the mind. This is not to say that 'money can't buy happiness', but using money without aim would create more damages than benefits. Wealth brings happiness as to be applied to connect to the higher spiritual values, especially the morality and human virtues and human that Buddhist economists have long-term value and fullness more than any material developments.

However, in social life, economic value is seen as happiness' basic, and also is a measure of an individual's achievements. Today, the caste system is gradually losing its influence, so everyone can do business; everyone has one's opportunity to create wealth and money in depending on one's ability. And to become an entrepreneur in the free economy, according to an economist, Liefaard Joop, CEOs want to succeed must meet four criteria: Vision, Knowledge, Enough is enough, and Courage.[1] In Vyagghapajja Sutta, the Buddha described to conduce to a householder's weal and happiness in this very life. Which four? "Achievement of persistent efforts (utthana-sampadā), the achievements of the care kidney (arakkha-sampadā), good friends (kalyanamittata) and livelihood balance."[2]

1. A good CEO is like the Bald eagle from high altitudes the bird tumble down in a dangerous free fall and very spectacular threw. The busines starting to full courage with confidence in one's ability to be proficient in the job, it can learn from the Bald eagle-flying high with its wings spreading. At this point, the Buddha also encouraged a householder doing successful livelihood by the persistent effort as a first courageous livelihood for proper means: "Herein, Vyagghapajja, by whatsoever activity a householder earns his living, whether by farming, by trading, by rearing cattle, by archery, by service under the king, or by any other kind

---

[1] Liefaard Joop, "4 Tips for The Successful Businessman"

[2] AN 8.54, Dighajanu (Vyagghapajja) Sutta: Conditions of Welfare

of craft -- at that he becomes skillful and is not lazy. He is endowed with the power of discernment as to the proper ways and means; he is able to carry out and allocate (duties). This is called the accomplishment of persistent effort.

2. A qualified CEO, in addition to his efforts, he also has a good vision or clear view on what is happening in the market for his vision and the market, such as the Bald eagle in the very high location, with its very sharp eyesight it has a clear view on the world below it and especially on the prey it want to catch, and avoid the dangers are lurking around it. Here, the Buddha also mentioned the achievements carefully; in addition, to the strength in oneself, a householder also must be properly and carefully vision in order to protect his assets from being destroyed: "Herein, Vyagghapajja, whatsoever wealth a householder is in possession of, obtained by dint of effort, collected by strength of arm, by the sweat of his brow, justly acquired by right means - such he husbands well by guarding and watching so that kings would not seize it, thieves would not steal it, fire would not burn it, water would not carry it away, nor ill-disposed heirs remove it. This is the accomplishment of watchfulness.

3. A smart CEO has extensive knowledge, knowing how to learn to adapt to habitat as same as a Bald eagle moving to seasonally appropriate environment, and can find its prey without encountering the dangerous cases. A skill businessman as a book, he should know about marketing and competitive techniques, clearly know their products and competitors, and also creating be connection with partners and build up the trust with his customers. Especially, with the knowledge he has,

he must have ethical standards in his business. At this part, the Buddha also suggested about wisdom for a householder being connected his 'good friends' to adapt to the social environment by engaging in discussions with the faith, virtue and wise to achieve the good livelihood in connection with the moral qualities of the community and the survival environment: "Herein, Vyagghapajja, in whatsoever village or market town a householder dwells, he associates, converses, engages in discussions with householders or householders' sons, whether young and highly cultured or old and highly cultured, full of faith (saddha),[4] full of virtue (síla), full of charity (caga), full of wisdom (pañña). He acts in accordance with the faith of the faithfulness, with the virtue of the virtuous life, with the charity of the charitable giving, with the wisdom of the wise. This is called good friendship. (Vyagghapajja Sutta)

4. A successful CEO who knows enough is enough in knowing how to restrict some products beyond his capability in produced goods and income. As Bald eagle catches one fish only at one point of time, but flying skills, its strong talons and its eyesight are extremely well developed capture a prey exactly. Here, the Buddha also advises a householder' success through livelihood balance. Without extravagant and stingy, he should know how his expenses and revenue, and limit the excess out of control for his stable and balanced life and not cause unfortunate crisis in any time which could smoked by others: "Herein, Vyagghapajja, a householder knowing his income and expenses leads a balanced life, neither extravagant nor miserly, knowing that thus his income will stand in excess of his expenses, but not his expenses in excess of his

income. Just as the goldsmith, or an apprentice of his, knows, on holding up a balance, that by so much it has dipped down, by so much it has tilted up; even so a householder, knowing his income and expenses leads a balanced life, neither extravagant nor miserly, knowing that thus his income will stand in excess of his expenses, but not his expenses in excess of his income.

"If, Vyagghapajja, a householder with little income were to lead an extravagant life, there would be those who say - 'This person enjoys his property like one who eats wood-apple.' If, Vyagghapajja, a householder with a large income were to lead a wretched life, there would be those who say -'This person will die like a starveling.'(Vyagghapajja Sutta)

According the four criteria above, the Buddha adviced wealthy householders how to preserve and grow their wealth and how to avoid the risk of loss of wealth. If richman only his own enjoyment, he would not be in harmony with society; society just reduce suffering and poverty when the rich man know how to share his assets. The lust for power and the excessive accumulation of wealth derived from uncontrolled craving; this has created a conflict and instability in the society through the resentment of the underprivileged people-who feel exploited by the effects of greed and (or) selfishness from others.

However, to avoid the risk of destruction and increase of wealth, the Buddha pointed out four main reasons in order to protect assets for a homeowner:

There are four sources of destruction of amassed wealth:

"(i) Debauchery, (ii) drunkenness, (iii) gambling, (iv) friendship, companionship and intimacy with evil-doers.

"Just as in the case of a great tank with four inlets and outlets, if a man should close the inlets and open the outlets and there should be no adequate rainfall, decrease of water is to be expected in that tank, and not an increase..."

There are four sources for the increase of amassed wealth:

(i) abstinence from debauchery, (ii) abstinence from drunkenness, (iii) non-indulgence in gambling, (iv) friendship, companionship and intimacy with the good.

"Just as in the case of a great tank with four inlets and four outlets, if a person were to open the inlets and close the outlets, and there should also be adequate rainfall, an increase in water is certainly to be expected in that tank, and not a decrease..." (Vyagghapajja sutta)

These four conditions are conducive to a householder's weal and happiness in this very life.

Thus, in Vyagghapajja sutta, besides the four conditions to preserve one's assets this life, the Buddha also mentioned the important conditions in the progress of spiritual 'assets' - which considered as baggage of happiness for our future:

There are four conditions to conduce to a householder's weal and happiness in his future life:

"The accomplishment of faith (saddha-sampada), the accomplishment of virtue (sila-sampada), the accomplishment of charity (caga-sampada) and the accomplishment of wisdom (pañña-sampada).

What is the accomplishment of faith?

"Herein a householder is possessed of faith, he believes in the Enlightenment of the Perfect One (Tathāgata): Thus, indeed, is that Blessed One: he is the pure one, fully enlightened...the teacher of gods and men..."

What is the accomplishment of virtue?

"Herein a householder abstains from killing, stealing, sexual misconduct, lying, and from intoxicants that cause infatuation and heedlessness…"

What is the accomplishment of charity?

"Herein a householder dwells at home with heart free from the stain of avarice, devoted to charity, open-handed, delighting in generosity, attending to the needy…"

What is the accomplishment of wisdom?

"Herein a householder is wise: he is endowed with wisdom that understands the arising and cessation of the five aggregates of existence; he is possessed of the noble penetrating insight that leads to the destruction of suffering. This is called the accomplishment of wisdom."

In conclusion, economic changes and the necessary structures require certain switching at the individual level. Economy and its development today aimed at strengthening and shaping its policies in global scale to combat poverty and global tensions. But the direction just show on the surface, instability inside is always hot issue on the media in every day. To me, opportunities for economic development should parallel with moral development, or the mind development, so may be more strong growth, sustainability and balance. As the Buddha said, the enlightened spirit comes from sense of connection with others and with the entire universe. This requires us to see our inner world in the great interdependence of the network of life, and we are one of the wires connecting together. That is also the view of impermanence and dependence, the enlightenment principles promote us in interacting with other people with more compassion and wisdom.

7.4 POLITICAL MORALITY

Political philosophy begins with the question: What is the relationship of the individual to society? How life can lead to good for humans? The themes seek to apply the environmental moral concepts and social environments connecting with the diversity of the forms of government and social existence that people can live harmonically; and so that, this also provides a standard to analyze and evaluate the existing institutions and its relationships. In the political field, the pragmatist will support the erection of the organization whose purpose is to ensure the greatest happiness for the greatest numbers.

Ethics is also strengthened by the metaphysical theory and epistemology, so the political views also concern the basic theory: the theory of the nature of reality and how we I know what a reasonable relation to the way we work, and how we interact with others. The Buddha, as well as Aristotle, was less concerned with the form of government rather than its consequences - the monarchy, democracy, aristocracy or any combination of a political regime - he just basically cares kindness and moral society that it serves.

The Buddha's political orientation started with educational methods. Society exists for understanding, sharing; ignorance is the root of all suffering. According to the Buddha, "human life is precious with opportunity and freedom." It is also a precious life of Kant's "dignity", and what Martin Buber called relation "I-Thou". To Buddha, All life is sacred beings and inconceivable.

In the paper of Buddha and politics, Maha Thera said, Gautama Buddha came from the warrior caste, and naturally had connections among the kings, princes and ministers. Despite the royal lineage and proximity to those who are in power, he never used the influence of the political power to promote his teachings and never allowed to abuse the teachings for gaining this political power. However, many politicians today are trying to use the Buddha's name for their own purposes, presenting him as a communist, capitalist or even imperialist. They have forgotten that modern political philosophy that we know now had actually appeared in the West after the Buddha's lifetime. Those who try to use the good name of the Buddha for their own benefit, must remember that the Buddha was perfectly awakened, standing above all worldly the concerns.[1]

However, the Buddha is a also a practical by his ideas promoting a social order in which everybody can be equal, and can live together peacefully. The Buddha encouraged that everyone ought to decrease person's desires and has more concerns the benefits for others. Although he didn't participate in the government, he has advised many kings, proposed universal health care, ecological activities and animal rights, and encouraged a development for merchant class in order to stimulate more advanced markets in personal connections. He is the first revolutionary class and misogynous prejudice of Hindu by allowing the low castes and women joined the Sangha.

The Buddha always encouraged the development of moral and spiritual issues depending on the material conditions of the society they live. He said that poverty is the cause of suffering and insecurity, and to contribute to growth for the instability and negativity of the society; a moral institution will create a fair society. Therefore, he encouraged the sharing for the poor people and the provision of economic

---

[1] Venerable K. Sri Dhammananda Maha Thera, "Buddhism and Politics"

justice from the leaders is indispensable to social harmony and political stability.

There is also an obvious and deep problem of mixing politics and religion. Fundament of a religion is purity, morality, faith, and wisdom while the fundament of politics is government. We know from history how often religions have been used in order to give more legitimacy to those who are in power and to justify their use of this power. When religion is used as an accomplice to the political caprices, it has to violate its original moral ideals and degrade under the influence of the worldly policy needs, which are very often egoistic. Exactly under these circumstances religion was used to justify wars and the seizures of foreign territories, and caused arrests, rebellions, violence, destruction of artefacts of art and culture, and so on.[1]

The Buddha's teaching is not aimed at creating new political organizations or making political decisions. In fact, Buddhism is trying to solve the problems of society through reforming those individuals who belong to it and provide the general principles on which society can be directed towards a greater humanity, improvement of its members' well-being and an equitable distribution of the resources.

There is a certain limit except for any political system can protect the welfare and happiness of the social members. No matter how perfect it may seem, this system would not be able to bring happiness and peace if its inside people still consist hatred, greed and delusion. According to Buddhism, compassion is the essence of the Buddha's political philosophy, and its development when we see the world is characterized by suffering (dukkha), and impermanence (anicca); and finally, we understand all of phenomena being equality and

---

[1] Ibid…

the absence of personality (anatman). The consciousness of selflessness is not denied to all but recognizing of the close interdependence (pratitya-samutpadha) between everyone and everything - no one can stand alone. With selfless enlightenment, we are able find themselves in others; personal happiness couldn't be separated from happiness of others. As seeing interdependence truth, we can develop our compassion, and show it actually.

Although a good and fair political system that guarantees human rights and has functions of control and balance of power is an important condition for a prosperous society, people do not have to waste their time seeking for the concept of the ideal system where citizens will be absolutely free. This is simply because there is no absolute freedom in any political system; it is only the mind that can be liberated. To be free, you need to look inside of yourself and manage bondages from the shackles of ignorance and craving. Freedom in the true sense is only possible when a person applies the Dharma teaching to development of him or her individually through righteous speech and actions, along with improving his or her mind, with an aim to realize its potential and achieve the ultimate goal, and of course, which is enlightenment.

While the benefits of the separation of religion from politics, along with the restrictions of politics in its ability to bring happiness and peace to the people, are quite obvious to Buddhist views. The Buddha is as the first revolution for political society when he spoke about the equality of all people before Abraham Lincoln did, and he taught that classes and castes are artificial barriers that had been created by society. In Aggañña Sutta, there is a paragraph that indicates that the classification is only based on people's morality from the three actions of body, speech and mind, which make the consequences of good and bad, pain or happiness, and so on: "And, Vasettha, a Khattiya who has led a bad life in body, speech and thought, and who has wrong view will, in consequence of such wrong views and deeds, at the breaking-up of the body after death, be reborn in a state of loss, an ill fate, the downfall, the hell-state, so this will a Brahmin, a Vaishya or a Shudra too."[1]

In other way, the Buddha maintained a spirit of a mutual support and participation in a society. This spirit is actively promoted in the political process of modern states. Although Buddhist monks are not involved in politics, in history, many lay people have participated in the political mechanism; they are the kings, presidents and state officials of the government. Thus, the Buddhist's political attitude includes of meaning and compassion, as the representation of the practical benefits for mostly people, and must be led in a spirit of selflessness and altruism.

Equally, no one has been appointed as the one who directly heirs the Buddha's tradition; the members of the community had to be guided only by the Dhamma and Vinaya (Buddhist monastic rules) in order to cultivate and achieve liberation in living of harmony. In addition to learning and meditation, they must know how to share Dharma teachings to the lay Budhists. In a life of purity and contentment, every member of Sangha owed no more than a bowl and three robes. Therefore, the Sangha is the ideal representative of the Buddhist's political philosophy.

Another aspect that is the Buddha supported of the exchange of views among everyone as in the traditional democratic process. According to Vinaya, every member of

---

[1] DN 27, Aggañña Sutta

this community has a right to contribute his (her) voice in its decision-making process. To solve any thing of the Sangha community, that based on the vote of more than half of its members. Thus, this particular element was reminded of of a contemporary parliamentary procedure in the democratic systems of the world which was in Buddhist monastic system in more than two thousand five hundred years ago. Today, political philosophy is pluralistic; on the needs and obligations of the groups the parties, and everyone has the right to vote for the one who he (she) loves. Buddhist community is also part of the powerful forces to elect for leaders who are rich wisdom and compassion, having ability to improve the life of society, environment, and sharing equal rights of happiness for everyone.

Buddhism ideally values in politics is morality and responsibility in using public influence and power. The Buddha did not accept any kinds of violence, and therefore the concept of war for justice is profoundly wrong. Buddha assured that both winner and loser are eventually suffering, and only the one who avoided the war is in peace. Moreover, the Buddha has even prevented a few wars between sixteen countries in his time (Dhammananda). Importantly, he considered for a governor to be uncorrupted and just, otherwise, he and his people would be unhappy. His words on this case are following: "Monks, when the ruler of a country is just and good, the ministers become just and good. When the ministers are just and good, the higher officials become just and good. When the higher officials become just and good, the rank and file become just and good. And, when the rank and file become just and good, the people become just and good." (from Jatakamala).

Therefore, the political values have practical significance in influencing and affecting people, and can change the human's problems and society rather than authority. Cakkavatti Sutta also contains the words of the Buddha about poverty as one of the basic causes of crimes, immorality, hypocrisy, fierce, hatred, and so on. All the defilements of mind can be caused by poverty, which is the result of centuries-old karmic history of humankind that brought those effects with its actions, are not easy at all to destroy with only the help of the governing power.[1]

The Buddha's progressive ideas in Kuṭadanta Sutta are the only possible compromise that can keep the human beings to maintain their lives in a more or less safe state. It is a suggestion that economic development, which will bring prosperity to all the classes of peoples, will be more effective in decreasing the crime level than any measures of punishment. In perspective, every human being must be provided with facilities of sufficient life, so that it could not only survive, but to save his or her moral dignity.[2]

In terms of social and political ethics, throughout history, moral values in the society are formed through historical and cultural events; however, each country was established by different principles and these principles will determine how a state will act in different situations. Also, to other progress in the field of international politics, the world organizations have rules they have to follow a certain direction. There are individual cases in accordance with their own principles but still have moral values; nevertheless, there are some topics that the members did not agree, or the principles of the members just got along to a certain extent, and then leading clashes in some perspective. For example, freedom of speech and press is preached by most countries, in fact, it

---

[1] DN 26, Cakkavatti Sutta

[2] DN 5, Kuṭadanta Sutta

changes from setbacks in other countries; As the Universal Declaration of Human Rights has not been applied yet for entire countries because some places are still in their conservative beliefs. The issues of moral reasoning in politics and society with certain principles are sometimes inconsistent; they vary from one place to another, from one region to other territories, because of different perceptions for them, and the various mechanisms in the current situation; for example, the right to freedom of expression may be in theory, but it change every day for the political features in fact. Ethics can be a political decision; however, when analyzing the effects of it, we should carefully consider its brilliant perspective in a certain situation.

Fundamentally, in Mahahamsa-Jataka there is a Buddha's list of ten rules of a good government (Dasa Raja Dhamma), which are still up-to-date in our times. Those rules require of a good ruler to be: "be liberal and avoid selfishness (1), maintainng a high moral character (2), be prepared to sacrifice one's own pleasure for the well-being of the subjects (3), be honest and maintain absolute integrity (4), be kind and gentle (5), leading a simple life for the subjects to emulate (6), be free from hatred of any one (7), exercising non-violence (8), practising patience (9), and respecting public opinion to promote peace and harmony (10)."[1]

Therefore, we can see that those considerations that Buddha has suggested concerning politics are not distinct among his other teachings. The fundamental truth is the same for the people included in political games and for those who is included in any other activities. Those are basic Buddhist's rules of morality, awareness, and dhyanas to overcome the hindrances and skillful deeds which make

---

[1] J534, Mahahamsa-Jataka

the linked composition of the Buddhist practical teaching. Obviously, The Buddha was a great reformer; for the field of politics, instead of discussing the reform of the polictic system, he only refers to the reform and transformation of personal inside. This is also a wake-wisdom (prajna) and compassion (karuna), which needed characteristics, can bring peace and hapiness for the world when everyone know how to govern transforming oneself befrore he or she want to lead the outside world in better way. The Dalai Lama said: "We can never obtain peace in the outer world until we make peace with ourselves."

8. CONCLUSIONS

As above, I have discussed The Buddha's doctrine implies all the domestic, social, economical, political, psychological, ecological spheres of life, as well as it concerns every element of universe in every moment of being. Especially, the aspects of the Buddha's teaching that can have an impact on the development of our modern society and that we can apply to improving our well-being in this world. The Buddha's main concern was liberating all the living beings from the non-ending circle of suffering that continues through our lives and deaths. Buddhism gave to us a vision, in which all the elements of universe are interrelated to each other in the cause-dependent origination, or the law of karma, that every action has its corresponding consequence, and we are all responsible for everything that happens with us.

The Buddha's worldview is not that pessimistic, because there is an inner happy ability to exit the shackles of suffering in every living being. Buddha does not say life is suffering; he just says the unenlightened life is suffering. In order to promote insight and create peaceful life for human and society, the Buddha has given the five precepts necessary for lay Buddhists to reinforce human virtues, and function of each precept would help people achieving true freedom from the consequences of anxiety and suffering if they adhere to certain principle. In the contemporary world, our minds easily polluted by the temptation of materialthe and scientific progress, are overflowing desires with the mental opacities that prevent us from seeing clearly and being happy. As everyone overpower negative desires by oneself, accordingly, he or she has chance of reduced suffering; seeing personal interests are also other interests, humans would not devastate the natural environment and the life with great love - instead of nurturing suspicion and hatred to mutual terror.

Attaching to all the passions of the ego, such as wealth and popularity, people are making harm to themselves and others, and in all circumstances, constantly searching for their ego through conceiving of six senses in contacting with six external objects. The Buddha was the only one who realized all that and moved far above the vanity and duality of the delusional reality most of us living in; according to the Buddha, the way to freedom is based on the principles of Wisdom and Compassion, which are qualities that can be reached through meditation and constant awareness to identify of our reality. There are moral precepts suggested by Buddha that are necessary to follow the right path, and there is a method, path itself, which is called the Noble Eightfold Path. This path consists of eight elements that can treatment for our mind and body, helping us to transform and free from suffering. The Noble Eightfold Path is also known as the Fourth Noble Truth or the Middle Way - between the extreme of sensual pleasure and self-mortification, between this and that, between eternalism và nilism, and so on. Enlightened middle truth, we gain tranquil and empty mind (S. 'Suunyataa, P. Sunnataa). In this state, it brings about dispassion and detachment by the gradual elimination of the desire for sensual pleasure; at this level, we also realize intrinsic value as a way of life, and led to the end of Dukkha, thus known as the state of Nirvana or the realm of be free from fears, so the characteristics of compassion and altruism are fully reflected.

And from a Buddhist basic point, the cause-effects laws are main working in all of life spheres throughout the three times: past, present and future, and a change and transformation just can come from within our minds. Our well-being, and health, along with the ecological condition of our planet will improve only when people knows how to limit their desires, to share their benefits to others, and constantly strive to perfect themselves to find really freedom from the bondages of negativity of three poisons by ignorant (avidyā/avijjā) leading.

Therefore, the Buddha's doctrine may be a great instrument applied in every sphere of our contemporary life because it is based on universal principles that invariably work, and be suitable for all of circumstances and human psychology. In wishes of compassionation, and along with positive development of mind qualities, so people will be able to overcome many obstacles by existential attitude and selflessness. Buddhism gives a clear worldview and instructions to achieve the state of inner freedom, and awaken our society from the endless suffering, also enlighten us with a pure wisdom and infinite compassion.

References

❖ *Avatamsaka Sutra (The Flower Garland Sutra), Practices and Vows of the Bodhisattva.* Dharmaflower.Net/ Samantabhadra.

❖ Beddow, Michael, *Digital dictionary of Buddhism*, 2010.

❖ Berzin, Alexander. *"Anger: Dealing with Disturbing Emotions."* (2003): n.pag.

❖ Billington, Ray, *Understanding Eastern Philosophy*, United Kingdom: Taylor & Francis, 1997, Print.

❖ Boisvert, Matthew, *"Pratityasamutpada (Dependant Origination)"* Encyclopedia of Buddhism, Ed. Robert E. Buswell. n.d. Print.

❖ Roderick Bucknell, Chris Kang (2013), *The Meditative Way: Readings in the Theory and Practice of Buddhist Meditation*

❖ Simon and Schuster, Johannes Bronkhorst (2009), *"Buddhist Teaching in India"*

❖ *"The Heart of the Buddha's Teaching"*, Parallax Press, 1998.

❖ *"Brahma Upanishad"* Coseru, Matthew, 2006

❖ Coseru, Christian, *"Mind in Indian Buddhist philosophy"* Stanford Encyclopedia. 12 Oct, 2012

❖ Dalai Lama and Howard C. Cutler, *The Art of Happiness in a Troubled World*, P Group (USA) Inc.

❖ Barua, M., & Basilio, A. (2009), *"Buddhist Approach to Protect the Environment in Perspective of Green Buddhism"* retrieved from http://mingkok.buddhistdoor. com/en/news/d/2471

❖ Damien, K. (2003), *The Nature of Buddhist Ethics*, New York, St. Martins Press.

❖ Sahni, P. (2008), *Environmental Ethics in Buddhism: A Virtues Approach*, Routledge Publishing

❖ Swearer, D. (2005), *An Assessment of Buddhist Eco-Philosophy*, Retrieved from http://www.hds.harvard.edu/cswr/resources/print/dongguk/swearer.pdf

❖ Yamamoto, S., & Kuwahara, V. (2009), *Symbiosis with the Global Environment: Buddhist Perspective of Environmental Education*, The Journal of Oriental Studies

❖ Der-lan Yeh, Theresa, *The Way To Peace: A Buddhist Perspective*, International Journal of Peace Studies 11.1 (Spring/Summer 2006).

❖ Dhammananda, K. Sri., *What Buddhists Believe.* 2005

❖ Francis, H. T., *The Jataka*, Vol. V: No. 534. Mahahamsa-Jataka, 1905

❖ Galbraith, John Kenneth S, *The Affluent Society*, New York: New American Library, 1963, Print.

❖ Ghose, Lynken, *"KARMA AND THE POSSIBILITY OF PURIFICATION: An Ethical and Psychological Analysis of the Doctrine of Karma in Buddhism*, Journal of Religious Ethics 35.2 (2007)

❖ Gomez, Luis O. *"Nirvana"* Encyclopedia of Buddhism, Ed. Robert E. Buswell. n.d. Print.

❖ Guruge, Ananda W. P., *The place of Buddhism in Indian thought*, n.d

❖ Kant, Immanuel, et al, *Critique of Practical Reason (Hackett Classics Series)*, Indianapolis: Hackett Publishing Company, 2002, Print.

❖ Leary, Timothy, *Neurologic*, 1973

❖ Melton J.G., Baumann M., *Religions of the World: A Comprehensive Encyclopedia of Beliefs and Practices*, Eds. Gordon J. Melton and Martin Baumann. 2nd ed. Santa Barbara, CA: ABC-CLIO, 2010, Print

❖ Nanasampanno, Acariya Maha Boowa, *Things As They Are: A Collection of Talks on Training of the Mind*, 1988, Trans. Thanissaro Bhikkhu, 1996

❖ Nikaya of Majjhima, Bhikkhu Nanamoli and Bhikkhu Bodhi, *The Middle Length Discourses of the Buddha*, 2009

❖ Page, Tony, *The Mahayana Mahaparinirvana Sutra*, Taisho Tripitaka 12.374 (2007): n.pag. Print

❖ Sangharakshita, *The Buddha's Noble Eightfold Path*, revised edition ed. N.P.: Windhorse Publications, 2007, Print

❖ Sarao, K. T. S. *"Anatman/Atman (No-self/Self)"* Encyclopedia of Buddhism. Ed. Robert E. Buswell. n.d.

❖ Shantideva, *Bodhisattvacharyavatara*, Trans. Stephan Bachelor, Dharmshala India: Library of Tibetan Works & Archives, 2015, Print.

❖ Soares, Theodore De Macedo, *The Twelve Nidanas*. n.d

❖ Story, Francis, *Foundations of Buddhism: The Four Noble Truths*, the Buddhist Publication Society 34/35. (2008): n.pag. Print.

❖ *The Buddhist Wheel of Life*, Dharmapala Thangka Centre. n.d.

❖ Tsongkhapa, Gareth Sparham and Shotaro Iida, *Ocean of Eloquence: Tsong Kha Pa's Commentary on the Yogacara Doctrine of Mind*, United States: State University of New York Press, 1993, Print.

❖ Vitanage, Gunaseela, *"Buddhist Ideals of Government"* Buddhist Publication Society Bodhi Leaf No. 11. (2011): n.pag. Digital Transcription Source: BPS Transcription Project

❖ Walshe, Maurice, O'Connell, *Mettam Sutta: The Brahmaviharas.* 2006

❖ Walter, Mariko Namba, *"Ancestors"* Encyclopedia of Buddhism. Ed. Robert E. Buswell. 2003 Print

❖ Willemen, Charles, *"Dharma and dharmas"* Encyclopedia of Buddhism. Ed. Robert E. Buswell. n.d. Print.

❖ Wittgenstein, Ludwig, et al, *Tractatus Logico-Philosophicus*: The German Text of Ludwig Wittgenstein's Logisch-Philosophische Abhandlung, 2nd ed. London: Routledge & Kegan Paul, 1922. Print.

❖ *"The Buddhist Monastic Code I"*: The Patimokkha Training Rules Translated and Explained, 2013, Web.

- http://dharmavoicesforanimals.org

- http://www.buddha-vacana.org

- http://www.accesstoinsight.org

- https://zh.wikipedia.org

- http://www.buddhanet.net

- http://secularbuddhism.org

- http://secularbuddhism.org

- http://www.chinabuddhismencyclopedia.com

- http://ccbs.ntu.edu.tw

- http://www.suttas.net